Political Parties in the Eighties

The American Enterprise Institute for Public Policy Research, established in 1943, is a publicly supported, nonpartisan, research and educational organization. Its purpose is to assist policy makers, scholars, businessmen, the press, and the public by providing objective analysis of national and international issues. Views expressed in the institute's publications are those of the authors and do not necessarily reflect the views of the staff, advisory panels, officers, or trustees of AEI.

Council of Academic Advisers

Paul W. McCracken, *Chairman, Edmund Ezra Day University Professor of Business Administration, University of Michigan*

Robert H. Bork, *Alexander M. Bickel Professor of Public Law, Yale Law School*

Kenneth W. Dam, *Harold J. and Marion F. Green Professor of Law, University of Chicago Law School*

Donald C. Hellmann, *Professor of Political Science and International Studies, University of Washington*

D. Gale Johnson, *Eliakim Hastings Moore Distinguished Service Professor of Economics and Provost, University of Chicago*

Robert A. Nisbet, *Resident Scholar, American Enterprise Institute*

Herbert Stein, *A. Willis Robertson Professor of Economics, University of Virginia*

James Q. Wilson, *Henry Lee Shattuck Professor of Government, Harvard University*

Executive Committee

Herman J. Schmidt, *Chairman of the Board*

William J. Baroody, Jr., *President*

Charles T. Fisher III, *Treasurer*

Richard J. Farrell

Richard B. Madden

Richard D. Wood

Edward Styles, *Director of Publications*

Program Directors

Russell Chapin, *Legislative Analyses*

Robert B. Helms, *Health Policy Studies*

Thomas F. Johnson, *Economic Policy Studies*

Sidney L. Jones, *Seminar Programs*

Marvin H. Kosters/James C. Miller III, *Government Regulation Studies*

Jack Meyer, *Special Projects (acting)*

W. S. Moore, *Legal Policy Studies*

Rudolph G. Penner, *Tax Policy Studies*

Howard R. Penniman/Austin Ranney, *Political and Social Processes*

Robert J. Pranger, *Foreign and Defense Policy Studies*

Periodicals

AEI Economist, Herbert Stein, *Editor*

AEI Foreign Policy and Defense Review, Robert J. Pranger and Donald C. Hellmann, *Co-Editors*

Public Opinion, Seymour Martin Lipset, Ben J. Wattenberg, *Co-Editors*; David R. Gergen, *Managing Editor*

Regulation, Antonin Scalia and Murray L. Weidenbaum, *Co-Editors*; Anne Brunsdale, *Managing Editor*

William J. Baroody, Sr., *Counsellor and Chairman, Development Committee*

Political Parties in the Eighties

Edited by Robert A. Goldwin

BRIAR CLIFF COLLEGE
LIBRARY
SIOUX CITY, IOWA

Jointly published by
American Enterprise Institute for Public Policy Research
Washington, D.C.
and
Kenyon College
Gambier, Ohio

Library of Congress Cataloging in Publication Data
Main entry under title:

Political parties in the eighties.

"Most of the essays in this volume were originally presented at a joint conference of the American Enterprise Institute and the Public Affairs Conference Center of Kenyon College."
1. Political parties—United States—Addresses, essays, lectures. I. Goldwin, Robert A., 1922– II. American Enterprise Institute for Public Policy Research. III. Public Affairs Conference Center.
JK2261.P64 324.273 80-14977
ISBN 0-8447-3382-2
ISBN 0-8447-3377-6 (pbk.)

AEI Studies 274

© 1980 by the American Enterprise Institute for Public Policy Research, Washington, D.C. All rights reserved. No part of this publication may be used or reproduced in any manner whatsoever without permission in writing from the American Enterprise Institute except in the case of brief quotations embodied in news articles, critical articles, or reviews.

The views expressed in the publications of the American Enterprise Institute are those of the authors and do not necessarily reflect the views of the staff, advisory panels, officers, or trustees of AEI.

"American Enterprise Institute" and (AEI) are registered service marks of the American Enterprise Institute for Public Policy Research.

Printed in the United States of America

JK
2261
.P64

6277849

CONTENTS

INTRODUCTION

American political parties have for a long time been a puzzle to the world, whether they are observed from a one-party system where elections are not free and never result in surprises, or from one in which real competition of programs and persons, with winners and losers every time, is as commonplace as in the United States. The puzzlement is genuine because, unlike parties elsewhere, ours have almost no program or platform uniting their members and distinguishing them from the opposition; impose almost no discipline on members once elected; have almost no continuing function between elections, whether in office or in opposition; and are not considered accountable, as parties, for the achievements or failures of incumbents. As a result, Americans, too, have great difficulty understanding and explaining what their parties are and what purposes they serve.

It is not surprising that there are always efforts afoot to change such parties, to strengthen or to "reform" them. Thirty years ago, there was an effort to make them more "responsible" and more centralized, with professional staffs to manage a continuing function and, thus, to ensure constructive participation by the party in governing as well as in campaigning. Since 1968, however, the trend has been in another direction. Changes in party rules have sought to democratize party activities, to diminish the influence of party professionals and elected officials, to rely more on primary elections for selecting candidates, and to guarantee greater participation by women and minorities.

The authors of the essays in this volume agree that the changes have affected constitutional processes profoundly, probably more so than do most constitutional amendments. But the authors agree on very little else. They disagree on whether parties have been improved or weakened in the last ten or twelve years, whether the selection process is now more democratic or less, and whether good candidates are more or less likely to be nominated and elected. More important, they disagree on the fundamental character of this political society and, therefore, on the kind of political party system that would best serve it.

The editor has sought to present the analyses and arguments of authoritative spokesmen of opposing views—as thoughtful, instructive, and responsible as could be found—but of such diversity that no reader could rationally agree with them all. The intention is to place the reader in the center of a controversy that is stated powerfully and argued with conviction. The reader who cares at all about great political issues has no alternative but to think for himself and to come to his own conclusions.

Most of the essays in this volume were originally presented at a joint conference of the American Enterprise Institute and the Public Affairs Conference Center of Kenyon College. Acknowledgment is gratefully given to Professor Robert Horwitz, then director of the Public Affairs Conference Center, for organizing the conference, and to Philip Jordan, president of Kenyon College, for his hospitable assistance. Acknowledgment is also due to William Schambra, assistant director of constitutional studies at AEI, for his editorial assistance in every stage of the preparation of this volume.

ROBERT A. GOLDWIN
AEI Resident Scholar

1

Party Reform: Revisionism Revised

Kenneth A. Bode and Carol F. Casey

The aftermath of the 1968 Democratic National Convention ushered in a decade of party reform that has been the subject of controversy since its inception. What critics fail to note, however, is that this contemporary reform movement grew out of a long tradition of American politics.

Since our founding fathers first promised government "which derives all its powers directly or indirectly from the great body of the people,"[1] the American political system has undergone a number of changes instituted by those who wished to add meaning to that phrase. Some of these were the results of gradual change, such as the evolution of Madison's factions into the formal mechanisms we know as political parties. Others were specific reforms designed to cure perceived abuses. Among these:

- Presidential nominations passed from the hands of congressional caucuses to national party nominating conventions.

- American blacks were guaranteed the constitutional right to vote after a bitter civil war and were assured the right to exercise that vote only after a hundred years of civil rights struggle.

- Women obtained suffrage early in this century and are still seeking to have their full rights recognized through a constitutional amendment.

- The election of U.S. senators became the direct responsibility of the voters, not the state legislators.

---

[1] Alexander Hamilton, John Jay, James Madison, *The Federalist Papers*, ed. Clinton Rossiter (New York: Mentor, 1961), No. 39, p. 241.

- The poll tax was banned as a prerequisite for voting.
- The direct primary was instituted in many states as a means of taking the nomination of elected officials from the party bosses and giving the responsibility directly to the voters.
- Apportionment for representative bodies was based on the principle of one man, one vote.
- The voting age was lowered from twenty-one to eighteen years of age for all federal elections.
- Most recently, campaign finance laws have been rewritten ostensibly to ensure against the abuses uncovered during the Watergate scandals.

In each instance, somebody gains power and somebody loses. In all cases, the justification for reform is some variation on two themes: broadening the base of political participation and holding public officials more directly accountable to the electorate.

Party reform was no exception.

If there can be said to have been a single, dominant theory behind the party reform movement of the last decade, it would be this: In a country in which two—and only two—political parties can elect a president, it is important that the nomination processes in both parties afford the possibility of a genuine test of the leadership and stewardship of candidates, even of an incumbent president. If such a test is precluded at the nominating stage, then the general election choice may be hollow for many participants.

The Democratic experience of 1968 clearly showed under circumstances of great stress that there was little accountability in the presidential nominating process. Party adherents who disagreed with their incumbent president on matters of major public policy had two very limited alternatives available to them: They could form a third party, or they could seek to influence the presidential nomination within their own party.

The first option was hardly viable. For more than a century, it has been evident that third-party movements have little chance to win the presidency. The American electoral system has increasingly institutionalized the two major parties as the only vehicles for obtaining office. In most states, the Democratic and Republican nominees—or the presidential electors designated on their behalf—are automatically and directly certified for ballot position in the November election. New and minor party candidates must mount a state-by-state effort to have their names placed on the ballot, a time- and money-consuming process usually involving the gathering of petition signatures under stringent procedural requirements within an extremely limited period of time. Although new and minor parties have won some gains in access to the ballot because of recent court cases growing out of George Wallace's 1968 presidential candidacy and Eugene McCarthy's 1976 presidential bid, those gains have been more than offset by public financing of presidential campaigns. Now, the Democratic and Republican presidential nominees are automatically given $20 million—adjusted for inflation—to mount their general election campaigns. In the nominating race, they benefit from the matching fund program, which doubles the value of every individual contribution of $250 or less. New and minor party candidates generally cannot reap these benefits, and if they can at all, it is only after the election is over.

In addition to the institutionalized bias in favor of the two-party system, the other obstacle to third-party success is the traditional pattern of voting behavior. Despite the growing number of Americans who claim to be "independents," the vast majority of these voters will cast their ballots for the major-party nominees. That was true when Maurice Durverger conducted his voting studies, and that remains the case today.

In 1968, the overriding issue for many Democrats was the Vietnam war. But those who sought to oppose President Johnson on this issue were often frustrated by structural barriers and procedural irregularities. Dissident Democrats, inspired almost entirely by opposition to the administration's Vietnam policies, were able to force Johnson's withdrawal. But because of Johnson's heavy hand on Humphrey's shoulder, along with the procedural chicanery the dissidents endured state-by-state during the caucuses and primaries, many of the 1968 insurgents were not attracted back into the party fold. The result was a Nixon victory and a serious examination of the party's nominating processes, which might not have otherwise occurred.

The earliest critics of party reform tended to judge the rules that came out of the successive Democratic party commissions only in terms of their ultimate result—the success of the party's presidential nominee in the general election—rather than viewing them in the broader context of the American political tradition. For the most part, the original eighteen guidelines adopted by the McGovern-Fraser Commission merely extended the concepts of fairness and equal protection to the presidential nominating process. These guidelines were developed in response to very real and serious flaws exposed in the tumultuous political arena of 1968. Without Vietnam, which divided the party so bitterly and stimulated previously inactive party members to attempt to express their opinions through the presidential nominating process, the party's internal decision-making processes probably would not have been subjected to such a close scrutiny. The year 1968 was not the first time that the party establishment had passed over the candidate with the best record in preferential primaries, in favor of a candidate of its own choosing. But in 1968, many who differed with the party establishment on issues and presidential candidate preferences found themselves deprived of an effective voice by a myriad of state laws and party traditions that worked against an election year challenge to an incumbent president.

Although the party reform rules are still hotly debated, mostly in academic circles, there is little attention to what the McCarthy and Kennedy supporters faced in 1968. The lessons they learned then bear repeating here.

In ten states, there simply were no rules: nothing whatsoever to regulate delegate selection procedures; to notify voters how, when, and where to participate in the presidential nominating process; and, most importantly, nothing to prevent party leaders from adjusting procedures when they found themselves under challenge. In at least ten additional states, rules existed but were inaccessible or grossly inadequate. In Rhode Island, for example, there were party rules, but it took a two-month search by the McGovern Commission (aided by U.S. Senator Claiborne Pell) to ferret out the single existing mimeographed copy from the files of a retired state chairman. Even where rules were readily available, important elements of the process were left to the discretion of local or state party officials. In Virginia, for example, mass meetings—the equivalent of precinct caucuses—constituted the first step of the process, and the only step generally open to rank-and-file Democratic participation. In 1968, the rules said that these were to be held sometime in April at a time and place determined by city and county committees and that notice was to be given in local newspapers. Seeking to turn out their supporters to these meetings, McCarthy organizers found that the typical notice was a small announcement in the legal section of the newspapers. Not infrequently, the mass meetings were convened on party-sponsored buses on the way to the state convention. Virginia party officials subsequently admitted that the most influential party reforms in their state were the requirements that meetings be held at uniform times and places and that adequate notice be given.

Missouri was one of the states with no rules at all. It also proved to be one of the most controversial battlegrounds in 1968 and provided a neatly contained laboratory for the McGovern Commission's analysis of the kinds of changes that might prevent a recurrence of the highhandedness and resulting divisiveness of that year. The only clues to the Missouri delegate selection puzzle were provided by the "Call to the State Convention," which left the dates, times, and places of ward and township conventions to each county chairman. The call was issued on April 15, 1968, and instructed each county to complete the first stage of the delegate selection process on or before May 3. As of April 30, according to the *St. Louis Post Dispatch*, seven of the eighteen townships in St. Louis County had made no arrangements for meetings, and, by the moring of May 3, the committeemen in four townships still refused to disclose to the newspaper the times or locations of the meetings they presumably intended to hold that day. In Concord Township, McCarthy organizers discovered the time and place of the meeting forty minutes before its scheduled beginning; by the time they arrived, the township convention was conducting its business.

At one township caucus, McCarthy supporters found themselves in a majority at the meeting, on the verge of electing some delegates. Suddenly, the party official chairing the caucus unpocketed 492 proxy votes—three times the total number of people in attendance—and cast them as a unit for his own slate.

At the other end of the state in Kansas City, a carefully selected list of party regulars (in many cases not the elected ward committeemen) received notices from Jackson County Chairman Frank Hughes instructing them to hold ward conventions at 8:00 P.M. on May 1, at places unspecified. Hughes published no notice of the time or place of these meetings nor of the persons he had designated as chairmen. On the night of April 29, he finally divulged his list of chairmen to McCarthy organizers, who then had to track down the chairmen on their own, to find out where the meetings would be held.

Where rules are vague, arbitrary fiddling with them is easy. This truth was not something new in 1968, of course. Four years before, Indiana's governor, a favorite-son stand-in for LBJ, lost one congressional district to Alabama's George Wallace. Embarrassed and chagrined, Indiana party leaders simply changed the party rules retroactively to provide that all delegates would be apportioned at large, thereby stripping Wallace of the convention delegates he had legitimately won.

Similarly, in 1968, rules were changed here and there. For example, in Comanche County, Oklahoma (home of Senator Fred

Harris, then Humphrey's national cochairman and later chairman of the Democratic National Committee), the rules were changed at the last moment. Only delegates selected at earlier precinct meetings could vote legally at the county conventions, but at the Comanche County convention, State Senator James Taliaferro moved that these rules be suspended and all registered Democrats at the meeting be permitted to vote. Packed in preparation for that motion, the meeting quickly changed its own rules, and, by so doing, rendered the results of the precinct meetings meaningless.

Proxy voting, as we have seen in the case of Missouri, was a device frequently used to disfranchise Democrats who had the perseverance to attend their precinct meetings. In Hawaii, proxies that provided the margin of victory at the state convention were later discovered to have come from an urban redevelopment area in Honolulu, precincts consisting largely of vacant lots.

In many other convention states, the use of the winner-take-all system ensured that successive majorities at each level of the process stifled discussion, dissent, and the representation of divergent points of view. In Iowa, Senator Eugene McCarthy received about 40 percent of the vote at the precinct caucus level. By the time the national convention delegates were chosen in June, that proportion had dwindled to around 8 percent.[2] Those in the majority at county and district conventions could—and did—elect all the delegates to the next level of the process. The ultimate result was that the presidential preferences of a substantial minority of voters were underrepresented or unrepresented at the national convention.

The late professor Alexander Bickel served as a consultant to the McGovern Commission and profoundly shaped some of its conclusions. Looking at the question of representation of minority views in the process by which delegates are selected, Bickel concluded:

> If at such preliminary stages in the delegate selection process successive majorities are allowed to prevail and to represent only themselves, and if the representation of minorities is not carried forward to the national convention, then it is quite possible, it is in some circumstances likely, that the final majority of delegates which prevails at the convention will represent a minority, and not a majority, of the Democratic voters in the country at large.[3]

---

[2] William Crotty, *Decision for the Democrats* (Baltimore: Johns Hopkins University Press, 1978), p. 45.

[3] Alexander Bickel, *Reform and Continuity* (New York: Harper Colophon Books, 1971), p. 54.

Even where the minority was permitted to elect some delegates to the convention at the next level, the imposition of the unit rule often prevented the expression of divergent points of view: a vote of the majority of the delegates at precinct and county conventions would bind all delegates—regardless of their presidential commitment—to vote for the candidate preferred by the majority. In Texas—the most notorious but by no means the only offender—the unit rule was applied in 224 of 254 county caucuses. In 1968, the unit rule was applied at Democratic party meetings in fifteen states using the caucus/convention system, including, besides Texas, Connecticut, Alaska, North Carolina, Tennessee, North Dakota, and several others.

Two primary states—Massachusetts and Oregon—had arrangements which permitted a unit-rule effect: delegates pledged to or favoring one candidate could be elected in a delegate primary and simultaneously be bound in a presidential preference primary to vote for an opposing candidate. In Oregon, Congresswoman Edith Green was cochairman of the Kennedy campaign and sought election as a delegate. She won, but Senator Eugene McCarthy carried the presidential preference poll, so Green was bound to vote for McCarthy at the national convention.

Other problems came to light in states with primaries in 1968. Fair representation of minority views was questionable in states that had winner-take-all primaries by statute (California, Oregon, South Dakota, Massachusetts, and Indiana), as well as those that were structured to have a district-by-district winner-take-all effect (Ohio, New Jersey, and Illinois).

In West Virginia, Illinois, Pennsylvania, Florida, New Jersey, and New York, primary laws permitted delegates to run with no notice to voters of their presidential preferences. How does a voter make an informed choice in a delegate primary, without knowing the candidates' stands on the central question before the convention? In New York, for local political reasons, the state law *precluded* candidates for delegate from listing a presidential preference. In other places, it was optional to list a preference, but official party slates traditionally ran uncommitted. In all these instances, the effect was essentially the same: Voters were required to cast a blind ballot.

In a number of other primary states—partially because of the divorce between popular presidential preference and selection of delegates with the blind ballot—the popular vote for a presidential candidate would have no bearing on the number of delegates won. In Pennsylvania, for example, Senator McCarthy won 78.5 percent of the preference vote, but only 24 of 130 delegates. The 52 at-large delegates had been elected three months before the primary by the state committee, well before any primaries or caucuses had been held anywhere in the country. And in the delegate primary, no presidential preference was listed by candidates. The result was a bitter party split and a credentials challenge on the charge that the delegation did not accurately reflect Democratic opinion in the state.

Democrats in other states faced even more serious barriers to participation. In Arizona, Arkansas, Georgia, Louisiana, Maryland, and Rhode Island, party members had no opportunity to participate in choosing their national convention delegates in the same year as the convention. In Georgia, the entire national convention delegation was chosen by the state party chairman, in consultation with the Democratic governor. In Louisiana, the governor made the choice, with the pro forma approval of the Democratic State Central Committee. In Arizona, Arkansas, Maryland, and Rhode Island, the national convention delegation was selected by party committees. Those committees, in turn, had been chosen in 1964 or 1966, thus denying the party's rank-and-file any voice in determining the 1968 presidential nominee. In fact, the McGovern-Fraser Commission found that, when Senator McCarthy announced his candidacy, nearly one-third of the delegates to the 1968 Democratic National Convention had, in effect, already been selected. By the time Lyndon Johnson announced his decision to withdraw from the presidential race, the delegate selection process had begun in all but twelve states.

The point of these observations is not that the McCarthy-Kennedy faction was discriminated against procedurally, nor that the deck was stacked against them—though in many instances they deeply believed that to be the case. The point instead is that, until 1968, one of the prime axioms of American politics was that a sitting president eligible for reelection could not be denied the nomination. The events of 1968 revealed some of the reasons this was so—reasons of rules and procedure extending beyond the vast patronage resources of the White House.

As the great battle for the nomination was being waged, another effort was being organized quietly. Challenges demanding some form of proportional representation were organized in Connecticut and Pennsylvania. A unit-rule challenge grew out of Texas. An apportionment challenge came from Minnesota. Objections were raised in Georgia to a racially imbalanced delegation hand-picked by the governor, and in Washington to delegates serving ex officio. Charges of racial discrimination or imbalance (or both) came from Mississippi, Georgia, and North Carolina. A loyalty oath challenge arose in

Alabama. Virtually every question raised in the subsequent deliberations of the McGovern Commission was anticipated in the credentials and rules challenges of 1968.

The rules battles of 1968 were initially conceived as a means of winning more delegates for Senator Eugene McCarthy at the convention in Chicago. But what began as a partisan scrap evolved into a lengthy, serious, often acrimonious analysis of the presidential nominating process by party commissions, academic committees, state legislatures, and Congress. An ad hoc party committee of Democrats including Alexander Bickel, Senator Harold Hughes, and Congressman Donald Fraser examined the complaints and abuses of 1968, made recommendations to the convention, and concluded that "state systems for selecting delegates to the National Convention display considerably less fidelity to basic democratic principles than a nation which claims to govern itself can safely tolerate."[4]

Viewed within the context of the time, the eighteen guidelines adopted by the McGovern-Fraser Commission were a moderate response to very real problems within the Democratic party's nominating process. Generally, they sought to apply the routine standards of fairness, due process, and equal protection enjoyed by voters in general elections to the internal decision-making processes of the party. Over time, the reforms have been adopted, codified, and implemented. They have also attracted a not inconsiderable body of critics, many of whom do not know or remember the genuine procedural abuses and abridgement of the democratic process that characterized the party of Lyndon Johnson in 1968. Like every other political reform in this century, party reform involved a certain redistribution of power. It became an extension of the partisan split of 1968 and prolonged the divisiveness of that year. Among those who were "distributed" out of power, those who argued backwards from outcomes they did not like, and those whose political theories were offended, certain myths about party reform have become conventional wisdom.

Myth No. 1: The reforms were devised by Senator McGovern for his own benefit and for that of the liberal-activist wing of the Democratic party.

A look at the composition of the commission is enough to defuse this myth. Senator McGovern was chosen to chair the commission by Senator Humphrey, who viewed Senator Harold Hughes of Iowa as too liberal and too closely identified with the McCarthy/Kennedy

[4] "Hughes Committee Report. The Democratic Choice," *Congressional Record*, October 14, 1968, p. E9172.

forces. Humphrey directed Senator Fred Harris, then National Democratic Chairman, to appoint McGovern. All appointments to the commission were made by Harris, a Humphrey backer, whose presidential ambitions were then tied to the Humphrey wing of the party. Commission members included three U.S. senators, one U.S. representative, four persons who were serving or had served as state party chairmen or vice-chairmen, one governor, one former governor, three current or past members of the Democratic National Committee, one state senator, one state treasurer, three labor union leaders, and two professors of political science. Overall, the majority of commission members were party regulars; most had supported Humphrey's 1968 presidential candidacy. As for McGovern, he knew no more about the presidential nominating process in fifty different states than did any other U.S. senator and proved to be an independent though somewhat tentative chairman, committed to democracy and fairness in party procedures, but dispositionally prone to compromise if the other side really dug in its heels.

It is conventional wisdom in some quarters that McGovern rigged the rules to his own benefit—some commentators even conjure a more elaborate scenario wherein the ouster of Mayor Daley from the 1972 convention was contrived years in advance—but they offer only their own phantoms for evidence. McGovern won the nomination not because the reforms gave him an edge but because in a span of less than a month he won primaries in New York, South Dakota, Oregon, California, Rhode Island, and New Jersey—all essentially unreformed, winner-take-all primaries conducted under the same rules as in 1968—and won thereby nearly half the votes he carried with him into the convention.

Myth No. 2: The membership of the commission is irrelevant: The important decisions were made by the commission staff—a staff dominated by young McCarthy/Kennedy political activists who had little regard for the Democratic party as an institution.

Consider for a moment what that says about senators like Birch Bayh, Harold Hughes, and George McGovern, about Governor Calvin Rampton of Utah and former Governor LeRoy Collins of Florida, or about politicians as good as Louis Martin, Warren Christopher, Will Davis, Fred Dutton, and George Mitchell, not to mention Adlai Stevenson of Illinois, and about professors as astute as Sam Beer of Harvard and Austin Ranney of Wisconsin. This group was led around by a couple of thirty-year-old political activists and a band of college interns? Although the staff and consultants did formulate the first draft of the guidelines based upon the information collected from seventeen regional hearings and additional research into each state's 1968 delegate selection system, few of the original guidelines remained intact after the commission had finished its deliberations. The staff proposals were debated at the commission's September 1969 meeting. Then the commission's revised guidelines were circulated to more than 3,000 Democrats, drawn from every list then available, for their comments before the final decisions were made in November 1969—after an additional two days of deliberation.

In the main, the commission had a pragmatic bent and a penchant for fairness. Confronted with a mountain of evidence that revealed flaws in the democratic process, they absorbed an overwhelming amount of detail in a short time about the ways fifty-four jurisdictions chose and mandated delegates. They fashioned practical, straightforward remedies.

The commission's most controversial guidelines were those requiring state parties to encourage the representation of women, blacks, and young people on the national convention delegation in reasonable relationship to their presence in the population—otherwise known as the quota system. These were purely the product of the commission itself. The staff draft contained no such guarantees, merely requiring affirmative steps to overcome the effects of past discrimination. The "quota" language grew out of a motion by Professor Austin Ranney, as expanded by Senator Birch Bayh, and adopted by the full commission.

Myth No. 3: The guidelines eliminated party leaders from the national convention delegations, thereby depriving the convention of their judgment and experience.

There is some truth to this charge: The commission did prohibit party committees or party leaders elected before the year of the national presidential nominating convention from selecting delegates, and it did limit selection of delegates by any party committee to not more than 10 percent of the national convention delegation. However, the ban on national convention delegates' being chosen by officials elected in an "untimely" fashion was merely a direct method of implementing the 1968 national convention's mandate; that mandate did not leave much leeway for interpretation. The 1968 convention said that delegates to the next convention had to be selected through "party primary, convention, or committee procedures open to public participation within the calendar year of the National Convention."

Those who argue that the new rules produced a lower-than-usual ratio of party and public officials in convention delegations tend to forget that politicians may have political reasons for avoiding party conventions. The list of those who did not show up at the 1968 convention contains many Democratic luminaries, including nearly all southern House Democrats who wanted to avoid any association with the national ticket. The list was long in 1972, too, in part because big-name Democrats in 1972 made an early swarm to the candidacy of Edmund Muskie. Not only were the big handicappers wrong, but so were the thousands of middle-level party regulars who went along with them and found themselves sidelined for the convention. In other words, the party's establishment was not at Miami Beach because they had backed the wrong horse.

Even so, data from the 1972 CBS convention survey indicates that the notion of the party convention without party leaders is largely the creation of the propagandists. Exactly one quarter of the delegates had held public office at one time or another, 38 percent had held party office, and 50 percent had been party officials at some time in their lives. Again, as evidence that the rules were not the problem, those same rules produced plenty of party leaders at the convention that nominated Governor Jimmy Carter in 1976.

The ignominy visited upon party leaders by the McGovern Commission guidelines was not that they were barred from participation, only that they were required to compete under the same rules as anyone else.

Myth No. 4: Reforms turned the nominating process over to activist elites whose views are unrepresentative of the total electorate, especially in states without primaries.

One of the fundamental objectives of the guidelines was to open the nominating process to broader participation. Particularly in convention states, the reformers were successful. Participation has jumped in every presidential nominating year so that caucus turnout now nearly rivals the average primary vote. Early results from the 1980 contest showed this trend: the Iowa Democratic precinct caucuses attracted nearly three times as many voters as they had in 1976. In Maine, turnout at the 1980 town caucuses was seven times as great as it was in 1976. Turnout has increased because Democrats have become more familiar with caucus procedures and because state Democratic parties have fulfilled their obligations of having published party rules, setting uniform times and dates for the first stage of the delegate selection process, and giving publicity to those events.

Critics, of course, contend that caucus participants are elites who do not represent the broader base of the Democratic party. Studies have shown, however, that those who attend caucuses are no more "elite" than those who vote in primaries. In both cases, persons with higher income and greater education are more likely to turn out. The same, in fact, is true in general elections. The reform rules are not to blame for the fact that participants in the presidential nominating process do not mirror the socioeconomic characteristics of the electorate as a whole. That is and has been true in every election held in the United States. The reform rules were designed merely to remove barriers to participation and give everyone equal access, not to guarantee advantages to any segment of the Democratic electorate.

Oddly enough, many of the persons who cry "elitism" also denigrate the party's affirmative action requirements as a quota system. The purpose of the outreach efforts imposed on state parties is to bring those groups that traditionally have low rates of political participation —blacks, Hispanics, and youth—into the active party ranks. Affirmative action (if it works) can only make the nominating process less elite.

What alternative do the "antielitists" offer? Basically, they suggest replacing one elite with another. Rather than permitting too much rank-and-file influence, they propose that elected Democratic party and public officials do a larger measure of the choosing. The professional functionaries of a party, notes Professor Bickel, maintain its continuity and play a role in its identity. Bickel goes on:

> The party's professional cadres should, no doubt, have a voice. The professionals are, if nothing else, a faction that deserves representation. Surely it is also sound institutional policy to reward their services with a measure of influence. Their greatest interest is the party's own institutional interest in winning—at least it is vouchsafed to them to see that interest over the long term. But if they lend the party its character of an "organized appetite" as Felix Frankfurter once wrote, their appetite is sometimes keener for power in the organization than for organizing to secure the power of government.[5]

It is also said the party professionals make well-informed and sophisticated judgments, tending to choose the abler rather than the more popular or glamorous candidate. When party leaders substitute their judgment for the popular view registered in primaries, however, they do not always produce winners. Stevenson was the leaders' choice over Kefauver, the primaries' choice, in 1952, as was Humphrey in 1968. Both lost.

[5] Bickel, *Reform*, pp. 41-42.

Myth No. 5: Reforms spawned primaries.

Some even argue more specifically that "the controversial rules changes that required a state's delegation to include minorities, young people, and women in proportion to their respective numbers in the state led directly to this proliferation of primaries. State party leaders fearing challenges to the makeup of their delegations, opted for primaries whose results conventions have traditionally been reluctant to upset."[6]

It is true that after the guidelines were adopted, many states enacted presidential primary laws. It is simplistic and inaccurate, however, to say that primaries were adopted *because* of the guidelines. Historically, the result of public dissatisfaction with acrimonious, divisive nominating contests has been the adoption of new primaries. Like it or not, primaries draw a favorable response from the general public. After the bitter Taft-Roosevelt battle in 1912, fourteen states instituted presidential primaries, bringing the total to twenty-six—a record that was not matched until 1976. After the Stevenson-Kefauver contest in 1952, states once again looked toward presidential primaries as a means of giving greater public legitimacy to the selection of delegates. Thus, the adoption of new primaries after 1968 is in keeping with the flux of American political history. By the time the McGovern Commission met for its first deliberative session in 1969, new presidential primaries had been introduced in nine state legislatures. Before the guidelines had been adopted, the number grew to thirteen.

The number of primaries has fluctuated in the past and is likely to do so again. The primaries adopted during the Progressive period were in response to a public desire to wrest control of nominations from the party bosses. Often the primary laws did just the opposite—maintaining control in the hands of party leaders, while providing the illusion of popular participation. In time, dissatisfaction with the way the primaries worked led to their abandonment.

There were a number of reasons why states opted for presidential primaries in 1972 and thereafter. In Maryland, for example, it was merely a case of returning to their usual system. Dismayed that George Wallace had won 43 percent of the 1964 presidential primary vote against LBJ stand-in Senator Daniel Brewster, and fearful that the Alabama governor could equal or better his showing in 1968, the Maryland Democratic party leadership abandoned the primary in favor of a committee selection system for 1968; they reinstituted the primary for 1972. In some instances, primaries are enacted to

[6] "Reform: What Works?" *Washington Post*, February 16, 1980.

benefit a potential presidential candidate. The Texas legislature adopted a primary law when Senator Bentsen threw his hat in the presidential ring. This primary was so obviously a vehicle for Bentsen that it carried a self-destruct clause after 1976. The North Carolina primary was to provide a vehicle for Terry Sanford. Georgia became a primary state when Jimmy Carter sought the nomination. In other instances, income and attention are motivating factors: The candidates, their campaigns, and the press who cover them are known to spend a great deal of money in "crucial" primary states. Vermont adopted a primary in the hope of a financial "spillover" from New Hampshire and Massachusetts. States established primaries in cooperation with each other to set up mini-regional primaries that would focus media and candidate attention more sharply on their regional problems. Because New Hampshire would not yield its "first-in-the-nation" status, the New England regional primary never became a reality. In 1976, a de facto western primary occurred when Idaho, Nevada, and Oregon all held their primaries on the same day. In 1980, the Southern regional primary occurred on March 11 when Alabama, Florida, and Georgia Democrats all went to the polls.

In 1972, New Mexico designed a presidential primary—distributing its convention delegates between the top two vote-getters—and scheduled it for the same day as the California primary, hoping for some attention. Most of the state's leading Democrats lined up behind Senator Humphrey. By primary day, the Democratic contest in California had boiled down to a Humphrey versus McGovern shootout for that state's winner-take-all lode of 271 delegates. Neither the candidates nor the press bothered with New Mexico. McGovern came in first and Wallace second in the voting; most of the party's leaders stayed home, and the next time around the state abandoned its primary.

Aware that many new primaries were resting in legislative hoppers around the country, the McGovern Commission went out of its way to stress that it had no preference between primary and convention systems, and that, run properly, either system could provide an open, democratic selection contest. It was no easier to comply with the guidelines by adopting a presidential primary law than it was to amend a party constitution to bring a state convention process into conformity with the rules. Using state law as an excuse for noncompliance did not protect a state, as Mayor Daley learned at the 1972 Democratic National Convention. The 9–0 Supreme Court decision in *Cousins* v. *Wigoda* underscores both the national convention's willingness to overturn primary results supported by state law and its right to do so.

In 1980, for the first time in more than a decade, caucus procedures are beginning to get a good press. Voters have discovered that the process is not intimidating and caucus states—at least the early ones—have begun to attract the kind of attention that once made primaries so appealing to party leaders who wanted a larger spot on the national tote board. There is no guarantee of it, of course, but we may be on the verge of another period when the appeal of primaries begins to wane and a more even balance with caucus systems is established.

In any case, the new, post-1968 primaries have assimilated reform requirements that make them more representative of primary voters and of Democratic party members. Presidential candidates now receive national convention delegates in proportion to the votes they win in the primary. Now, only Democrats can vote in Democratic presidential primaries. When voters cast their ballots for candidates seeking to be convention delegates, they know which presidential aspirant the candidate supports. These are significant accomplishments when measured against the type of primaries that were held in 1968 and before.

Myth No. 6: Proportional representation is a notion of European origin that will fragment the American party system, exacerbate divisions, prolong the nominating contest, and make unity more difficult.

The early winnowing of the field in 1976 and the subsequent unity behind Jimmy Carter's nomination took much of the air out of this balloon. Common sense suggests that those who lose a fight fairly will be more likely to rally around the eventual winner than those who lose because they think the deck was stacked against them. Contrast 1976 with 1968.

Myths such as these have clouded a thoughtful evaluation of what party reform did, in fact, accomplish. The rules provided a convenient battleground for a spirited factional dispute within the party. The debate seemed to encourage exaggerations like the current notion that the reforms have made the contest so long and exhausting that only candidates without jobs can compete—witness Jimmy Carter and Ronald Reagan in 1976; George Bush, John Connally, and Reagan again in 1980. Candidates with a lot of time on their hands could do well under the old system, too, as Richard Nixon proved in the two years before 1968. And, as far back as 1959–1960, John Kennedy's attendance record in the Senate got no gold stars.

It is also said that the addition of twenty new presidential primaries has weakened the party system and that primaries are a bypass mechanism that saps the parties' vitality. If this is true (which it may not be), then the place to look to remedy the weakness is at the base of the pyramid where tens of thousands of municipal, county, district, and state primaries determine nearly every nomination of every party in the country.

Parties are getting weaker. Anyone would concede as much. But they have been eroding over the course of the past century, as David Broder points out in his perceptive study, *The Party's Over.* Public financing of elections, the movement of candidates away from political parties as organizing mechanisms to garner support in the electorate, the influence of television on our politics and its use in supplanting party organizations in get-out-the-vote drives—these, much more than the addition of a few presidential primaries, have been responsible for the weakening of the party system over the past decade.

After the revisionist bombast is cleared away, a few things become clear. First, the original McGovern reforms have undergone two lengthy, thoughtful reviews by follow-up party commissions not predisposed to accept the reforms as gospel. There have been some modifications, some tinkering, but the basic concepts that guided the original reform proposals have been endorsed by both commissions. Ninety percent of the original guidelines have been accepted and codified into party rules around the country. In 1980 we may see the second consecutive hard-fought presidential nomination conferred without procedural bitterness—not a bad accomplishment after 1968 and 1972. In other words, the basic principles of the reform movement have been accepted, and they are with us to stay.

Second, the people seem to be going for the reforms. Participation is up in both parties. In an era of cynicism about parties, a *Los Angeles Times* poll (December 16–18, 1979) found that 70 percent of Americans nationwide said the nominating system was "basically sound," compared with 62 percent for the political system as a whole and only 49 percent for the judicial system.

Finally, those who condemn the party reforms as too radical must at least concede that they headed off worse possibilities. Public opinion polls throughout the late 1960s and 1970s showed whopping majorities of Americans cynical about political parties, politicians, and institutions, and strongly in favor of a national primary, abolition of the electoral college, and establishing a binding national initiative.

The survival of political institutions lies in their adaptability. Party reform is the latest evidence of that.

2

Party "Reform" in Retrospect

Edward C. Banfield

It can hardly be believed how many facts naturally flow from the philosophical theory of the indefinite perfectibility of man or how strong an influence it exercises even on those who, living entirely for the purposes of action and not of thought, seem to conform their actions to it without knowing anything about it.

Alexis de Tocqueville

In a paper written almost twenty years ago, I maintained that a political system is an accident, and that to meddle with one that works well is the greatest foolishness of which men are capable.[1] Nevertheless, I said, a democracy will always meddle, because its logic legitimates only such power as arises from reasonable discussion about the common good in which all participate. A democracy will therefore try to reform away all power from other sources and—since power arising from reasonable discussion is never enough to govern—democracy must eventually reform itself out of existence. My argument referred especially to the American party system, which had produced good results precisely because of its alleged defects, that is, its lack of correspondence to the democratic ideal. Eliminating these "defects," I concluded, might "set off changes that will ramify throughout the political system, changing its character completely."

I put the word "reform" in quotation marks to call attention to its misuse by those who think any change that aims at improvement is a reform even if it makes matters worse. Properly speaking, a change is a reform only if it makes matters better in the manner intended. As Burke said in his *Letter to a Noble Lord*, "to innovate is not to reform."

1 "In Defense of the American Party System," *Political Parties, U.S.A.*, ed. Robert A. Goldwin (Chicago: Rand McNally, 1961), pp. 21-39. Reprinted as an appendix in this volume.

In this essay, I begin by describing the changes (most of them unintended and unwanted consequences of efforts at reform) that have occurred in the national party system. I turn then to a consideration of how these changes in the party system seem to have affected the political system as a whole, conjecturing that the changes have indeed ramified and may prove to have changed the character of the system completely. Finally, I show that it was mainly the "logic of the democratic ideal" that brought about the changes.

The "Old" Party System and the "New"

In the days of the "old" party system—from Andrew Jackson's time to about the mid-1950s—both national parties were loose confederations of state parties that came alive every four years to nominate presidential and vice-presidential candidates and then to wage campaigns for them. Some state parties existed in name only, but most were loose alliances of city machines, state and local officeholders, labor unions and other interest groups, and some wealthy individuals.

To be taken seriously as a contender for the presidential nomination, one had to be a leading figure in a major state party organization or have the backing of someone who was. The state leaders, many of whom were governors or senators, were political professionals who typically had worked themselves into positions of power by faithful service to the party. A few party leaders in each state, usually in some sort of convention—a "smoke-filled room"—chose the state's delegates to the national party convention.[2] To win the presidential nomi-

---

In this section I have relied heavily upon data from (in alphabetical order): Herbert E. Alexander, *Financing Politics* (Washington, D.C.: Congressional Quarterly Press, 1976); Herbert B. Asher, "The Media and the Presidential Selection Process," in *The Impact of the Electoral Process*, vol. 3, ed. Louis Maisel and Joseph Cooper (Beverly Hills/London: Sage Electoral Studies Yearbook, 1977); Jeane Jordan Kirkpatrick, *Dismantling the Parties* (Washington, D.C.: American Enterprise Institute, 1978); Everett Carll Ladd, Jr., *Where Have All the Voters Gone?* (New York: W. W. Norton, 1978); Gary R. Orren, "Candidate Style and Voter Alignment in 1976," in *Emerging Coalitions in American Politics*, ed. Seymour Martin Lipset (San Francisco: Institute for Contemporary Studies, 1978); Gerald M. Pomper, "The Decline of Partisan Politics," in *The Impact of the Electoral Process*, ed. Maisel and Cooper; Austin Ranney, *Curing the Mischiefs of Faction* (Berkeley: University of California Press, 1975); and Austin Ranney, "The Political Parties: Reform and Decline," in *The New American Political System*, ed. Anthony King (Washington, D.C.: American Enterprise Institute, 1978).

[2] This does not necessarily mean that the state party leaders failed to choose the most popular candidates. William H. Lucy has shown that since 1936 (when polls began), the active candidate who led the final preconvention poll was nominated nineteen of twenty times (Lucy was writing in 1973) and all but two of these nominations were on the first ballot. "Whether under the old procedures or the

nation, therefore, an aspirant had to put together a winning coalition of state leaders. If he happened to be the party leader, perhaps the governor, of a large state, he would have as many as 15 percent of the number needed to win "in his pocket"—obviously a considerable advantage in the coalition-building process. Early in the present century, some states, in response to complaints of "bossism," substituted the direct primary for the convention as a way of choosing delegates. (In 1916 at least twenty-two states had presidential primaries, but the number had declined to about sixteen by 1936.) However, state conventions, which is to say state party leaders, chose well over half the delegates as recently as 1952, and therefore safely controlled the nominating process.

The nominee of a major party could be sure of a substantial vote even if he did nothing but sit on his front porch until election day. Most voters "belonged" to one party or the other and would vote almost automatically for the candidate of their party. In the 1950s, about 90 percent of those in national samples identified themselves with a major party.

Having come to life to nominate its candidate, a national party remained active long enough to raise and spend money on his campaign. In the days before radio, it relied mainly on meetings with oratory, full-page advertisements in the big-city newspapers, leaflets, brochures, buttons, and direct mail (in 1912 postcards went to each of the 1.6 million voters in the state of Pennsylvania). The national parties sometimes gave subventions to state and local party organizations to pay for house-to-house canvassers, whose main job was to see that the party regulars got to the polls.

Being the choice of a winning coalition of state party leaders, the candidate who made it to the White House would bring with him the support of at least some key figures in the House and Senate. He could never be a real party "boss"; the separation of powers and the traditional congressional distrust of the president prevented that. He could, however, exert a good deal of influence (for example, on the selection of House leaders). As V. O. Key remarked in the first (1942) edition of his famous textbook, "the party system, when it operates properly, overcomes the handicaps to governance imposed by the

new, the relationships since 1936 between polls, primaries, and nominations are consistent with the view that presidential politics have tended toward national publicity and moved away from reliance on factional alliances and tangible incentives as means of winning the nomination." "Polls, Primaries, and Presidential Nominations," *Journal of Politics*, vol. 35 (1973), pp. 837, 847.

separation of powers and furnishes a common leadership and a bond of loyalty by which the President and Congress may work together."[3]

A president could take it for granted that he would be renominated for a second term. If he had lost his popularity with the country or had antagonized a powerful faction of his party, he might have some opposition, but, because of the favors his administration could give or withhold in the states and because the state party leaders would consider it disastrous for the party to repudiate its leader, he could have his way if he insisted. (From 1860 on, the only elected presidents not renominated for a second term were two who declined—Hayes in 1880 and Roosevelt in 1908.)

That was the "old" party system. The "new" one is strikingly different. Today an aspirant for the presidential nomination need not be a state party leader or have the support of one. What is essential today is that he show promise of being able to win an enthusiastic, but not necessarily overwhelmingly large, popular following.

This change results from a sharp increase in the number of states having presidential primaries: from seventeen in 1968 to thirty in 1976. Now nearly three-fourths of the Democratic and more than two-thirds of the Republican convention delegates are chosen in primaries. Even in the states that retain the convention system, party leaders are not as free as before to choose—and control—delegates. Obviously, a would-be nominee will court voters, not party leaders. If he does well enough with the voters, he may have the nomination won weeks before the convention is called to order.

His problem being to show that he can win primaries, the aspiring candidate will need to build an organization suitable for that purpose—one or two advisers with a talent for this sort of entrepreneurship, and several technical specialists: fund raisers, pollsters, direct mail advertising experts, television and radio producers, organizers of volunteers, legal advisers, and so on.

Since all this will cost a lot, the candidate will, a year or so before he announces his candidacy, file with the Federal Election Commission the names of the members of an "exploratory committee" which will make the preliminary arrangements necessary to establish his eligibility for government preconvention campaign funding. (To be eligible, he must have raised $5,000 in contributions of $250 or less in each of twenty states.) Under present regulations, a candidate for the nomination may raise and spend $2.2 million for fund raising and another $5.5 million for campaign expenses. He may not accept indi-

[3] *Politics, Parties and Pressure Groups* (New York: Thomas Y. Crowell, 1942), p. 520.

vidual contributions of more than $1,000. The government will match contributions of $250 or less per person up to a total of $5.5 million. Thus his preconvention expenses may be as much as $13.2 million. (If he elects to spend his own money, the law imposes no limit.)

As he moves from one primary to the next, the candidate is followed by a troop of newspaper and television reporters and cameramen. Much depends upon them. They are, as David Broder has remarked, "talent scouts" and "handicappers."[4] If a columnist says that a candidate's prospects are improving, that may help them to improve, for the report may bring more contributions, more volunteers, and more attention from the media, the effect of which may be to improve his standing in the polls, which in turn may reinforce the opinion that his prospects are improving, which in turn. . . . In the same way, of course, a reporter's impression may set the candidate's campaign on a downward spiral and bring it to an untimely end.

In making his appeal to primary voters, the candidate will consider very carefully just how partisan to be. He knows that about one-third of all voters—one-half among the young—disclaim any party affiliation. If he campaigns as a strong party man, he may drive many of these "independents" into the arms of his opposition in the general election. Even with the voters who belong to his party he must watch his step: if he lets himself be embraced too warmly by a state party leader, he may be charged with being a tool of the "bosses." In some primaries, cross-over voting is allowed: that is, a voter registered in one party may have the right to vote in the primary of another. The turnout in primary elections is small (usually from 25 to 35 percent of those eligible). Since what the candidate needs is a small but dependable army of enthusiasts, his rational strategy may be to make a conspicuous display of his independence by attacking the regulars of his own party. "Insurgency," Gerald Pomper has written with reference to the campaigns of Reagan, Carter, and Brown, "is no longer the crusade of political Don Quixotes; it is the most likely path to the political kingdom."[5]

Once nominated, the candidate—not the party—is eligible to receive a flat grant of government funds for his general election campaign expenses. (The party will have received a government grant, but only for convention expenses.) If he accepts the federal funds, as he almost certainly will, the candidate may not spend, or coordinate the spending of, any other funds. His party, however, may spend up

[4] Cited by Asher, "The Media," p. 213.

[5] "Decline of Partisan Politics," p. 28; see also Orren, "Candidate Style," pp. 146-51.

to two cents per voting-age citizen (about $3.2 million) on his behalf. Individuals and groups—corporations and labor unions, for example—may spend as much as they please provided their activities are independent of his.

The newly elected president is not likely to be on close, cordial terms with the leaders of his party in the House and Senate. They and the other state party leaders had no part in choosing him as the nominee, and he had very likely been at pains to keep a certain distance from them during the campaign. From their standpoint, he may be an "outsider," even an "amateur." If the president and his party's congressional leadership overcome the handicaps to governance imposed by the separation of powers, it will obviously not be because the party system has furnished "a common leadership and a bond of loyalty."

Under the "new" system, the president cannot count on renomination. On the contrary, he must expect to fight for it and, perhaps more often than not, to lose. He will have a considerable advantage in the new round of popularity contests because of the constant attention he has been given by the media. On the other hand, he will be held accountable for whatever has gone wrong. That rather small and unrepresentative part of the public that votes in primaries is likely to have lost enthusiasm for him, since it is impossible for him to have done all that the enthusiasts expected from him in office. But even if the polls show there is little chance of beating him, some will try. With government financing of campaigns, there is little to lose, and of course there is something, if only notoriety, to gain.

Some Consequences for the Political System

The party system is, of course, a component of the larger set of arrangements that is the political system. It is characteristic of any system that its elements are interrelated in such a manner that a change in the state of any one produces changes in all the others. "Reform" of the party system may therefore be expected to produce changes in features of the government that are in a sense remote from the parties themselves.

How has the political system been affected by the movement from the "old" to the "new" party? The question does not admit of a really satisfactory answer. For one thing, it is impossible to specify the particular causes, very likely many and diverse, that together have produced a particular effect; party "reform" was certainly a contributing cause of some changes, but how can one say whether its contribution was large or small? For another thing, the effects in question are seldom readily apparent; they may appear at unexpected places within the political system and at unexpected times: the most important may not appear for many years, until some unusual strain is put upon the political system.

Obviously, then, the list that follows must be regarded with much caution. It is a set of conjectures, the plausibility of which the reader will have to judge.

1. The near exclusion of state party leaders from the process by which presidential candidates are selected has gone far toward transforming the American political system from one of representative to one of direct democracy. As contrived by the Founders, the system distributed power among a numerous and intricately graded set of authorities who spoke for, and helped to form the opinions of, diverse publics. The Founders meant government to be responsive to widely shared, strongly held, and informed opinion, and they looked to the leaders of the many publics to organize and express this opinion.[6] State and local party leaders came in time to be among the most effective of these leaders.

These and other intermediate authorities having become fewer and less influential now, "public opinion" has become more and more what the individual, who may neither know nor care about the matter at hand and who need feel no obligation to consider the public interest, says in response to questions framed by the Gallup Poll or put before him or her in the privacy of the voting booth. Obviously, there is more reason now than there was in 1789 to fear that direct democracy —the democracy whose opinion is prepared by the newscaster and recorded by the pollster—will fail to produce governments capable of protecting the society from enemies foreign and domestic.

2. Insofar as democracy is direct rather than representative, people must be held in civil discipline by one central authority rather than by numerous intermediate ones. As the power of these other authorities declines, that of the central one must increase. The new

[6] "Washington did not believe that it was either possible or practical to supply the people in advance with the information that would enable them to advise wisely before a decision was made. And after the decision, they would first have to be persuaded that the issue was adequately grave to command their deepest attention. Then, so that they would not come up with vaporous ideas, they would have to be made to understand what were the possible alternatives. They would have to be given time to study the matter. If the people then expressed in some finite manner—through a spontaneous flood of mass meetings or through the ballot box—disapproval of the government's actions, it would be 'disgraceful' for the government not to follow their lead." James Thomas Flexner, *George Washington*, vol. 4 (Boston: Little, Brown, 1972), p. 480.

power must come from different sources than the old and will therefore be of a very different character. Whereas local authority derived largely from respect for persons and institutions whose qualities were known more or less at first hand, central authority must depend essentially upon the arts of mass merchandising—on "image" rather than character. As a presidential public relations adviser remarked not long ago, what matters is less the content of policy than the way it is packaged. In this change, two dangers are apparent: first, that in order to generate the power it must have to govern, the central authority will come to neglect serious deliberation in favor of hasty generalization or "the trick of rapidly framing and confidently uttering general propositions" creating "levity of assent"; second, that this trick will succeed too well and tyranny will result.[7]

3. The "new" system makes probable the election of a president who is radically unacceptable to a substantial majority of the electorate. Under the "old" system, there was always the likelihood that mediocrities would be nominated: one could be confident, however, that they would be *moderate* mediocrities—the party professionals would see to that. Now it is likely that unrepresentative enthusiasts, voting in primaries, will produce extremist candidates in both major parties. Even if, under the pressures of office, the elected extremist adapts to the realities of the situation by moving toward the center, the consensual basis on which freedom and order so critically depend may in the meanwhile have been badly damaged.

4. The changes in the party system have decreased somewhat the power of the presidency in relation to that of the Congress. A president under the "new" system normally will not enter the White House as

[7] The quoted words are from Sir Henry Sumner Maine, *Popular Government* (New York: Henry Holt, 1886), pp. 106-8. In my article cited above, I recalled Maine's observation that party and corruption had in the past always been relied upon to bring men under civil discipline but that now (1886) a third expedient had been discovered:

> This is generalization, the trick of rapidly framing, and confidently uttering, general propositions on political subjects. . . . General formulas, which can be seen on examination to have been arrived at by attending only to particulars few, trivial or irrelevant, are turned out in as much profusion as if they dropped from an intellectual machine; and debates in the House of Commons may be constantly read, which consisted wholly in the exchange of weak generalities and strong personalities. On a pure Democracy this class of general formulas has a prodigious effect. Crowds of men can be got to assent to general statements, clothed in striking language, but unverified and perhaps incapable of verification: and thus there is formed a sort of sham and pretence of concurrent opinion. There has been a loose acquiescence in a vague proposition, and then the People, whose voice is the voice of God, is assumed to have spoken.

the leader of a coalition that includes principal figures in the House and Senate and, as often as not, he may be an "outsider." Under the best of circumstances, it takes some time for a new president to establish the basis of understanding and trust with the leaders of his party in Congress on which the success of his efforts at leadership depends. His position vis-à-vis Congress—indeed, vis-à-vis all those with whom he must deal—is much weakened by the fact that he may fail to win renomination: a president who has, say, a 25 percent chance of serving for eight years will presumably be taken only half as seriously as would one who has a 50 percent chance. The possibility of challenging the president for the nomination will be ever-present in the minds of some key figures in Congress. This will make it all the more difficult for the president to exert leadership there. Those who see themselves as possible challengers will refrain from supporting presidential positions they may later want to attack. The president, knowing that his strongest party associates are potential opponents, will avoid using them in ways that might improve their standing in the polls.

5. The diminution of the president's influence with the leaders of Congress has opened new opportunities for the exercise of influence by special interest groups. This, in some measure, explains the phenomenal increase in the number of Washington lobbies in the past thirty years—from about 2,000 to about 15,000. (The main cause, however, has surely been the extension of federal intervention into every nook and cranny of national life.) Insofar as the competitive bidding of interest groups replaces presidential leadership, the policy outcome will be delay, stalemate, and contradiction. Government will be more "conservative," that is, less able to act, but the flood of special interest legislation will continue to rise. Presidential influence would be needed to stop it—more influence now than in the "old" days because congressmen who once depended upon the party label and the party precinct captains to keep them in office must now look elsewhere for the large sums needed to court the issue-oriented voter. (The average House chairman received $45,000 from political action committees in the 1978 elections.)

6. Public confidence in and respect for government will decline. The "new" system gives members of the president's party the incentive to undermine confidence in him and in his administration, in the hope of taking the nomination from him. There is a limitless supply of grounds (albeit mostly technical) for charging violation of the campaign financing laws and therefore "corruption." An "outsider" president will be unable to establish his ascendancy over other party

leaders. There will be an appalling increase in the amount of special interest legislation and a relentless thrust of the bureaucracies toward self-aggrandizement. These and other causes will make the citizen ever more angry and frustrated with government and ever less disposed to think of it as the defender of liberty and justice.

The Accidents of "Reform"

The transformation of the "old" party system into the "new" happened largely by accident. No one intended the old system to be weakened, let alone dismantled. On the contrary, the intention of the reformers was to strengthen it by making it more democratic.

One very important set of "reforms" was made possible by court decisions which transferred power to make rules for delegate selection from the state parties and legislatures to the national conventions. Half a century before, reformers had given up as hopeless ideas which, because of the changed attitudes of the courts, now became practical. In the exercise of its newly won power, the Democratic National Convention did not mean to substitute primaries for conventions nor to exclude state party leaders from the process by which presidential nominees were chosen. The eighteen "guidelines" proposed by its Commission on Party Structure and Delegate Selection and revised by two subsequent commissions, were intended only to encourage participation, especially by women, young people, and members of minority groups, in all stages of the process. It was clear that some contenders for power, especially those associated with Senator George McGovern, would gain by this. The intention of the reformers, however, was to make the process of selection more democratic.

That the transfer of power from the states to the national conventions would cause many state party leaders to withdraw entirely from the delegate selection process was not foreseen. It is safe to say that none of the reformers of 1968 guessed that in less than ten years, a candidate would win the nomination well before the convention. It is safe to say, too, that none of them realized that by greatly increasing participation in the selection process (from 11 million in 1968 to 30 million in 1976) they might bring about the choice of a nominee less representative of the party rank and file than one chosen by a few party professionals.[8]

[8] Austin Ranney has said that the purpose of those who framed the new rules for the Democratic party in 1969-1972 was "not to make the party more combat-ready" or to make it more representative "of all elements of the New Deal coalition" and "certainly not of party notables or regulars or contributors." The

Another important set of "reforms"—those relating to campaign finance—were intended to make the system more democratic by eliminating from elections, so far as was feasible, the special influence of wealth. Public funding of the candidates, so it was thought, would guarantee nearly equal opportunity to all. That the Supreme Court, by striking down key sections of the law on First Amendment grounds, would actually increase the relative importance of "professional" contributors (interest groups of all sorts) and of "family giving" by the rich, could not have been foreseen. It seems highly implausible, on the other hand, that the professional politicians did not realize they were grievously damaging the parties by voting to give campaign funds to candidates rather than to parties. Yet, the record seems to support this view.

The "reforms" of the late 1960s and early 1970s were the culmination of more than a century of efforts to bring party politics into correspondence with the democratic ideal. The ruling elite always favored—in principle if not in practice—a politics that would settle issues on their merits rather than "give everyone something." The ethos of this elite, toward the end of the nineteenth century, inspired the municipal reform movement, whose program included nomination by petition as well as the initiative, recall, and referendum. From city government, the reformers moved to state government: open primaries were adopted (as was noted above) by many states in the early years of the twentieth century. Apparently it was the impossibility of establishing uniform rules for selection of delegates under the legal doctrines then prevailing that caused many reformers to lose enthusiasm for presidential primaries.[9]

The nonpartisan style of the elite steadily diffused into the middle class. As incomes increased and more and more boys and girls went to high school and even to college, the size of the middle class grew both absolutely and in relation to the working class. All those who had read a civics book knew that "bosses" were always "corrupt" and that the enlightened citizen would vote for "the best man regardless of party." In the 1930s and 1940s there was (judging from the polls) no ideological difference between the college-educated and others. There seem to have been, however, marked differences in political style. The relatively well-educated were made uncomfortable

reforms, he writes, "were intended to maximize the representation of 'purists,' not of 'professionals.'" "Comment on 'Changing the Rules Changes the Game,'" *American Political Science Review*, vol. 68 (March 1974), p. 44.

[9] Robert C. Brooks, *Political Parties and Electoral Problems* (New York: Harper and Brothers, 1923), p. 279.

by Harry Truman's affinity for professional politicians of the Kansas City variety and by his unabashed partisanship; at the same time they were respectful of Dwight Eisenhower's "man above party and above faction" stance and admired Adlai Stevenson's elegant superiority to the party "hacks." In 1952 and again in 1956, these two candidates, each in his own way, strengthened the already widely held view that parties were obsolete.

The Republican party was gravely damaged by Eisenhower's neglect. The Democratic party was hurt by Stevenson in an altogether different way. Enormously attractive to young liberals, he inspired many of them to try to enter party politics in the large cities in the hope of democratizing it. The "amateur democrat," as James Q. Wilson described the type in the early 1960s, "sees the political world more in terms of ideas and principles than in terms of persons. Politics is the determination of public policy, and public policy ought to be set deliberately rather than as the accidental by-product of a struggle for personal and party advantage. Issues ought to be settled on their merits."[10] It was the "amateur democrat," moved now to the national scene, who, following the 1968 convention, devised and won acceptance for the "guidelines" that brought the Democratic party close to the democratic ideal and close, as well, to destruction.

In 1960 amateurs of a different sort demonstrated how little the party professionals had come to matter. The nine men who met at his father's Palm Beach home to plan a strategy for John F. Kennedy's nomination were not party leaders: they were relatives, friends, and employees (only one was a professional politician)—persons attached to him as a person, not as a party figure. At that time, only eleven states chose all their convention delegates in primaries (four others chose some). Accordingly, Lawrence F. O'Brien went on the road to tell the key state leaders of the candidate's qualities. The main thrust of the Kennedy strategy, however, was not in this direction; rather, it was to make a showing in the polls and the primaries. Television, which had begun to reach mass audiences early in the Eisenhower years, had now come of age, changing the situation fundamentally by making it possible for a candidate—albeit only for one who was well-financed—to address the voters over the heads of the party leaders.

Appealing over the heads of the party leaders would have done a candidate no good in the "old" days of strong party loyalty and strong precinct organizations. It was because partisanship had declined sharply that Kennedy could use the media with great effect. (In 1960

[10] *The Amateur Democrat* (Chicago: University of Chicago Press, 1962), p. 3.

only 21 percent of the Survey Research Center's sample of voters identified themselves as "strong" Democrats; 33 percent were either "weak" or "independent Democrat," and 8 percent were outright "Independent.") Kennedy's success may therefore be viewed, in large part, as a consequence of the decline of partisanship that had long been underway.

This decline is sometimes accounted for in part by the greater salience to voters in the 1950s and 1960s of issues—especially race, the Vietnam war, and the environment—that bear little relationship to the historical bases of Republican-Democratic division: namely, taxes, employment, farm prices, and the like. This is plausible. It is likewise plausible that causality may have run in the opposite direction as well: that the weakened attachment to party was a necessary and perhaps sufficient condition of the emergence of the new issues; parties, both as organizations and as bodies of received wisdom, may have functioned to "decide" what was, and what was not, to be the subject matter of politics. There is still another possibility. Both phenomena—the decline of partisanship and the salience of the new issues—may be effects of a single cause: the general moralization of public life that has followed from mass acceptance of views that once were the exclusive possession of an educated elite.

The Prospect

A good many politicians, journalists, and even some political scientists have begun to think twice about the wisdom of the "reforms" that have been made in the party system; there is widespread agreement that the parties have been seriously weakened without being made more democratic. No one, however, proposes trying to undo the damage to the parties by (for example) restoring control over the selection of convention delegates to the states or by ending government funding of campaigns. The reason for this is not that the damage cannot be repaired (although clearly the "old" system cannot be put back together again); rather, it is that such proposals would not be taken seriously. Enthusiasm for pressing further and faster toward direct democracy remains unabated. Further changes are being made in the Democratic party's delegate selection rules to "wipe out the last vestiges of the 'winner-take-all' system,"[11] government funding of both House and Senate campaigns is under active consideration in Congress, support is growing for a constitutional amendment to

[11] *New York Times*, February 25, 1979, p. 17.

establish a national presidential primary (a Gallup Poll has found that the public favors popular election of the president by five-to-one), and Senate hearings have been held on bills to amend the Constitution to provide both the referendum and the initiative.

There is a deep irony in the fact that, during the Bicentennial period in which we celebrate the achievement of the Founders, we also complete the undoing of it. The system that they established was based explicitly upon the understanding that man is a creature more of passions than of reason, that the problem of the lawgiver is to find ways of holding him in check, and that this can be done only by making ambition counteract ambition. It was based also upon the consequent understanding that government must have limited objects: to promote the life, liberty, and the pursuit of happiness of its citizens, *not* to right all wrongs. The fundamental fact of today is that man is seen, not as he is, but as he ought to be. Liberalism, which in one version or another has become our civil religion, imagines that he is above all reasonable and therefore capable, through the acquisition of knowledge (actually information and technique), of solving all problems and of progressing toward perfection. So long as this delusion persists, we shall be impelled to reform out of existence—at whatever cost to civilization—not only the "defects" of our political system but whatever else may, or may seem to, impede the establishment of heaven upon earth by the exercise of reason and good will.

3

The Undemocratic Party System: Citizenship in an Elite/Mass Society

Benjamin R. Barber

If I could not go to heaven, but with a party, I would not go there at all.

Thomas Jefferson (before he became the first great leader of the Republican party)[1]

The Party System and Representation

A raging controversy, of which this volume is but a restrained instance, has enveloped the party system in America. The debate has turned on such questions as whether democracy is best served by a regional or a national party system, by a state convention or primary system for presidential nominations, by traditional machine party politics or "democratic" people's party politics, by personality- or issue-oriented political campaigns—in short, by old-style party politics or new-style reform party politics.

It is my contention here that the controversy is in one sense fundamentally irrelevant to the issues it affects to raise. The simple fact is that party government and the representative system to which it belongs are both deeply inimical to real democracy and have evolved from the outset, to no small degree by design of the Founders and early practitioners of our political system, in a fashion that has consistently diminished rather than enhanced self-government.

There is without doubt a crisis of sorts afflicting party government. James MacGregor Burns described it fifteen years ago as a

[1] Jefferson, like so many of the Founders, can easily be cited on every side of an issue. His fondness for rural democracy, ward government, and individual rights must be balanced against the strong party leadership and executive authority he exercised in his presidential years.

"deadlock of democracy" in which the congressional and presidential branches of the major parties created a four-party system that paralyzed national leadership and the effective use of power for national policy making.[2] More recently, a venerable pundit has alluded to "the near collapse of the party system,"[3] while the inability of President Carter to treat with a Congress controlled by his own party suggests systemic as well as personal problems for the president as party leader. Meanwhile, but a third of the eligible electorate votes, and a third of those are without any party affiliation.

Yet much of this crisis has been precipitated by the incompatibility of representation itself with full freedom, equality, and social justice. A well-known cautionary adage has it that the voter under representative government is free only on the day the ballot is cast. But even this act is of dubious moment in a system where, although millions share the franchise, it is used only to select the few who exercise every other duty of civic importance in the nation. To exercise the franchise is unfortunately at the same time to renounce it. The representative principle steals from individuals all significant responsibility for their values, beliefs, and actions; ultimately it turns them into passive clients of party bosses (the old elite under the old elite party system) or active pawns of public opinion manipulators and their well-packaged national leaders (the new elite under the new mass party system). In neither case is there any real question of self-government—only a dispiriting choice between direct elite rule or elite rule via the masses, between elite persuasion and mass persuasion (Nelson Polsby's choice in this volume), between rule by party hacks and rule by popular demagogues, between backroom politics and editorial page politics.

The vital political idea of citizenship eludes completely the sociological (and hence unpolitical, even antipolitical) terminology of elite and mass. Modern parties, construed in this alienating language, leave no room for citizens understood as self-governing community participants. It is no accident that the mainstream tradition of American social science has concerned itself not with The American Citizen, but only with The American Voter,[4] voters being as far from citizens

[2] *The Deadlock of Democracy: Four-Party Politics in America* (Englewood Cliffs, N.J.: Prentice-Hall, 1963), pp. 324-25.

[3] Richard Strout ("T.R.B."), *The New Republic*, May 26, 1979.

[4] All the classical electoral studies of the 1950s and 1960s focus on the voter rather than the citizen; see, for example, P. Lazarsfeld, B. Berelson, and H. Gaudet, *The People's Choice* (New York: Columbia University Press, 1948); A. Campbell et al., *The Voter Decides* (Evanston, Ill.: Row, Peterson, 1954); and most recently, N. H. Nie et al., *The Changing American Voter* (Cambridge: Harvard University Press, 1979).

as spectators are from participants or patients are from the doctors they select to heal them.

The startling and dismaying truth is that those who have entered the debates about the democratic or undemocratic implications of the American party system either do not believe in democracy or do not understand it. Conservative critics of party reform presumably follow in James Madison's footsteps, perceiving in large, democratically controlled, majoritarian parties a clear and present danger to stable and prudent government. To them, party reform must appear as another instance of that "excess of democracy" against which Samuel P. Huntington sounds a tocsin in his bicentennial essay, "The Democratic Distemper."[5] They no more believe in popular rule than did their forebears like Alexander Hamilton who espied in the people only a voracious and dangerous "Beast." Their concern is with prudent rulership not participation, the protection of private rights not the pursuit of public purposes, limited government not active citizenship; hence they view democracy at its best only as a possible means to other primary ends. In Martin Diamond's emphatic description: "*democracy was only a form of government* [for the Founders] *which, like any other form of government, had to prove itself adequately instrumental to the securing of liberty.*"[6] In this framework, the traditional elite party model obviously seems a safer, if less democratic, bet than the reform model.

The reformers appear to be democrats, and they do appeal explicitly to popular sovereignty and accountability in assailing the traditional elite party system. Jefferson was perhaps the first of such reformers, his "supreme achievement as a party leader" having been to "reach out to embrace new voters," giving majority rule "a more popular, egalitarian impetus" and creating a "vigorous, competitive party, under strong leadership."[7] Yet few of his heirs seem to have grasped that within the confines of a representative system which, in Schumpeter's characterization, allows the people only to select among

[5] *The Public Interest*, no. 41 (Fall 1975), pp. 9-38. Huntington's particular biases are evident in these passages: "The effective operation of a democratic political system usually requires some measure of apathy and non-involvement on the part of some individuals and groups. . . . Marginal social groups, as in the case of the blacks, are now becoming full participants in the political system. Yet the danger of 'overloading' the political system with demands which extend its functions and undermine its authority still remains." (p. 37.)

[6] "The Declaration and the Constitution: Liberty, Democracy and the Founders," *The Public Interest*, no. 41 (Fall 1975), p. 47, emphasis in original.

[7] Burns, *Deadlock*, pp. 33, 41.

the elites competing to govern them,[8] attempts at democratization tend to diminish the prudence and attenuate the moderateness of rulership without increasing its accountability or enhancing the quality of participation and citizenship. As George Bernard Shaw scoffed, one can "substitute selection by the incompetent many for appointment by the corrupt few," but it is not at all clear that the latter is any more democratic than the former if thoughtful, autonomous, community self-government is to be the measure of democracy. The problem apparently lies not in the insufficiently democratic character of the reformers' wish to democratize, but in the intrinsically undemocratic character of the larger representative system to which both traditional and reform party politics belong.

This system is much less hospitable to the three most cherished values in American political life—freedom, equality, and social justice—than is generally perceived. It is incompatible with freedom because political will is alienable only at the cost of self-government and autonomy, because, as Rousseau warned in *The Social Contract*, "the instant a people allows itself to be represented it loses its freedom,"[9] because freedom and citizenship are correlates, each sustaining and giving life to the other, because women and men who are not directly responsible through common deliberation, common decision, and common action for the policies that determine their common lives are not really free at all—however much they enjoy rights of privacy, property, and individuality.

Representation is incompatible with equality because, in the astute words of the nineteenth-century French Catholic writer Louis Veuillot, "When I vote my equality falls into the box with my ballot—they disappear together";[10] because equality construed exclusively in terms of abstract personhood or legal and electoral equity omits the crucial economic and social determinants that shape its real-life incarnation, because equality without community is not only a fiction that can divide as easily as it unites but, in the form of *Gleichschaltung*, it offers the dread specter of a mass society of indistinguishable consumer clones.

Finally, representation is incompatible with social justice because it encroaches on the personal autonomy and self-sufficiency that every

[8] Cf. Joseph Schumpeter, *Capitalism, Socialism and Democracy*, 3rd ed. (London: George Allen & Unwin, 1950), pp. 269-83.

[9] *Oeuvres complètes* (Paris: Editions Gallimard, 1964), vol. 3, book III, chap. 15, p. 431, my translation.

[10] Cited by Robert Michels, *Political Parties: A Sociological Study of the Oligarchical Tendencies of Modern Democracy* (Glencoe, Ill.: Free Press, 1915; reprinted, 1949), p. 39, my translation.

moral order demands, because it incapacitates the community as a self-regulating instrument of justice and destroys the possibility of a participatory public in which the idea of public justice might take root.

Freedom, equality, and justice are in fact all *political* values that depend for their conceptual coherence and their practical viability on self-government and citizenship. They cannot be apprehended, let alone practiced, by clients or by pawns; they are not to be found in the lexicon of either elites or masses. They are the special province of citizens, and unless some way is discovered to represent citizens without annulling citizenship, all party government—in its traditional and its reformed versions—will continue to obstruct rather than serve them.

Centrifugal and Centripetal Tendencies of Elite/Mass Party Organization

It can be said, in defense of the party system, that the device of representation was precisely the solution the Founders offered to the problem of rendering democracy workable in a large-scale republic, a way of addressing the dangers of faction and anarchy without falling prey to the perils of unaccountability and tyranny (whether popular/majoritarian or elite). As Madison had put it, the representative system could "refine and enlarge the public views by passing them through the medium of a chosen body of citizens,"[11] thereby achieving a delicate balance of popular control *and* prudent government, participation *and* effective national administration, accountability *and* centripetal efficiency. Political parties, in turn, as they evolved piecemeal from the administrations of Jefferson and Madison through those of Martin Van Buren and Andrew Jackson, became the chief institutional means through which the representative principle was established in American political life. They were (to appropriate Bagehot's phrase) the buckle linking governmental authority to the people in whom authority had its theoretic origin, linking elite and mass in a continuum that made voters the ultimate yet passive arbiters and the elite the active but dependent governors of the nation's political life.

Parties were rooted in the populace, thereby securing the people from abuse by their governors; but parties were at the same time insulated from the people, thereby securing the government from

[11] *The Federalist,* No. 10 (New York: Modern Library, 1964), p. 61. The representative system is among the institutions discussed in their original constitutional setting in my "The Compromised Republic," in *The Moral Foundations of the American Republic,* ed. R. H. Horwitz (Charlottesville, Va.: University of Virginia Press, 1977), pp. 25-26 et passim.

abuse by the people (manifested as popular prejudice, majority tyranny, and mob caprice). Party government held the promise of a temperate democracy, one which, even when tried by populist and progressive excesses and stretched by mass manipulators or near demagogues (Jackson? Roosevelt? Kennedy?), could mediate the anarchic factions and the tyrannical majorities that would inevitably accompany the growth of American democracy. That at least was the theory, the hope, the faith of our skeptical republican forefathers.

For all this, there is not much in the historical experience of American political parties, and still less in the political theory of party government as argued in the tradition from Edmund Burke to Robert Michels, to demonstrate that parties have made good or can make good on this faith. Quite aside from the fundamental problems representation raises for democracy, parties bring with them their own liabilities both for self-government and for central administration. I contend that parties are afflicted both with radical centripetal (elitist) tendencies and with radical centrifugal (disintegrative or anarchic) tendencies which together undermine their utility as mediating devices between authority and the public and thus their viability as saving compromises in the service of popular democracy.

Both tendencies have long been well-known to critics of political parties, and little is offered here that has not been largely anticipated in early English and American discussions. Yet because both the old guard and the reform movement seem united on the intrinsic merit of the party system and at odds only over the character of that system, a number of the earlier arguments may bear rehearsal.

Perhaps the most searching as well as the most sweeping critique of the centripetal tendencies of party government came at the beginning of this century in Robert Michels's elaboration of the iron law of oligarchy in the context of party. To Michels, the evolution of representative democracy is inherently unstable, following a "parabolic course" that, however promising the democratic beginnings, leads inevitably to oligarchy. Moreover, these "oligarchical and bureaucratic tendencies" are a "matter of technical and practical necessity" since they are an "inevitable product of the very principle of organization."[12] This suggests natural limits to representative democracy of a far more severe kind than usually attributed to pure or participatory democracy. Michels concurs with Rousseau in insisting upon "the logical impossibility of the 'representative' system, whether in parliamentary life or in party delegation."[13] If "the will of the people is not transferable,

[12] *Political Parties*, p. 33.

[13] Ibid.

nor even the will of the single individual," then clearly "the first appearance of professional leadership marks the beginning of the end."[14] Victor Considérant, a forerunner of Michels, offers this striking metaphor: "In delegating its sovereignty, a people abdicate it. Such a people no longer governs itself but is governed. . . . Turning Saturn on his head, the principle of sovereignty ends up being devoured by its daughter, the principle of delegation."[15]

In the particular French Left examples he had before him, Michels was witness to what he saw as the typical democratic attempt to maintain popular sovereignty by "subordinating the delegates altogether to the will of the mass, by tying them hand and foot," as well as to the failure of this attempt. Mandate representation inevitably gives way to specialization, expertise, organization, bureaucracy, and leadership so that, albeit power "issues from the people, it ends by raising itself above the people."[16] Michels's bitter conclusion was this:

> Under representative government the difference between democracy and monarchy, which are both rooted in the representative system, is altogether insignificant—a difference not in substance but in form. The sovereign people elects, in place of a king, a number of kinglets. Not possessing sufficient freedom and independence to direct the life of the state, it tamely allows itself to be despoiled of its fundamental right.[17]

Unhappily, this form of criticism, because it is associated with neo-elitist and left-anarchist ideology of a distinctly nineteenth-century variety, has been largely ignored in America. Pareto, Mosca, Michels, Proudhon, Malatesta, and Considérant are hardly fashionable elders of American social and political science. Yet there is much in the history of American party evolution that confirms Michels's tough analysis by exhibiting the centripetal tendencies of party government. For one thing, every attempt at countering party elitism in America has run afoul of the nation's Lockean consensualism. As Louis Hartz and Daniel Boorstin have effectively argued, this consensualism has been a permament barrier to the kinds of ideological polarization and doctrinal party programs that might otherwise have been used to secure through an obligatory mandate popular control over government. Where parties have upon occasion been rendered more ideological

---

[14] Ibid., pp. 33-34.

[15] *La solution, ou le Gouvernement direct du Peuple* (Paris: Librairie Phalansterie, 1850), pp. 13-15, my translation.

[16] *Political Parties*, p. 38.

[17] Ibid.

and programmatic, the result has often been intraparty breakdown and electoral failure rather than greater democracy (the Goldwater and McCarthy campaigns are prime examples in recent decades). Even proponents of democratic reform (Donald M. Fraser in this volume, for example) acknowledge that the great efforts at democratizing the Democratic party of 1968 through 1972 did more to weaken and fragment than to democratize it; constituencies were polarized and a variety of interests given expression, but the party did not end up with a clear mandate. The Carter presidency has suffered in part because of the incoherence left behind by those heady years.

For the most part, however, party government in America has pretty much followed the Michels script. The requisites of effective leadership and a winning electoral strategy have created party bosses and machine politics at the local level and party hierarchy and presidential hegemony at the national level. Modern life with its demands of specialization, efficiency, and expertise has compounded the difficulties. As Michels astutely foresaw:

> It becomes more and more absurd to attempt to "represent" a heteronomous mass in all the innumerable problems which arise out of the increasing differentiation of our political and economic life. To represent, in this sense, comes to mean that the purely individual desire masquerades and is accepted as the will of the mass.[18]

Party government is then prone to centripetal elitism because party government is government by *leaders*, and as Burke rightly understood, while leaders are "faithful watchmen . . . over the rights and privileges of the people," their "duty" is to "give them information, and to receive it from them"; a leader cannot "go to school to them, to learn the principles of law and government."[19] The people are thus at best *voters* when they choose their leaders and *clients* when they are served diligently by them. They are not citizens in either capacity, and cannot be.

Nonetheless, it can fairly be argued that the evolution of American party government has followed a cyclical rather than a parabolic course, that political parties have alternated between elite and popular

---

[18] Ibid., p. 40.

[19] *Burke's Politics: Selected Writings and Speeches of Edmund Burke*, ed. Ross J. S. Hoffman and Paul Levack (New York: Alfred A. Knopf, 1949), p. 219. Of course Burke at this point sounds rather like James I, who insisted likewise he was not to be instructed by the public in "my craft. . . . I must not be taught my office." Cited by Samuel Beer, *Modern British Politics* (London: Faber & Faber, 1965), p. 6.

(or mass) models. Unfortunately, as my brief discussion of reform may suggest, this qualification (if true) does not moderate the centripetal tendencies of party; it only provides an equal centrifugal tendency, equally undermining to stable democracy. The centrifugal tendencies of representative government are most visible during periods of populism, progressivism, and reform when rank-and-file voters are trying to reclaim their parties from ossified elite leadership. Voters insist on being taken seriously, demand that neglected interests be articulated and served, and take control of their party either through programmatic party platforms or institutional and procedural modifications that permit more input into the process of leader selection. But at no point do such changes transform voters into self-governing citizens or permit clients to see themselves as self-responsible agents. Communities are not established, interests are promoted. Consequently, although the intent is to return government to the public at large, such reforms generally return it to this or that particular public—Michels's "purely individual desire masquerading as the will of the mass." The public at large, however, remains even more fragmented and privatized than under elite leadership (where, in deference to the Burkean principle, leaders at least attempt to attune themselves to cross-sectional, national, and occasionally even truly public purposes).

Once again, there is little here that would have surprised Burke or Rousseau or indeed the Founders. The polarizing and tyrannical disposition of popular prejudice (what then went by the name of popular opinion) when given the force of a representative franchise was a constant concern of almost every great political theorist from Montesquieu through John Stuart Mill and Tocqueville. Madison made the problem of faction the centerpiece of his first *Federalist* paper (Number 10), and saw in it the greatest single threat to the stability of republics. He anticipated almost every conceivable abuse of popular party politics of the putatively "democratic" variety when he wrote there: "Men of factious tempers, of local prejudice, or of sinister designs, may, by intrigue, by corruption, or by other means, first obtain the suffrages, and then betray the interests of the people."[20] Public opinion turns out to be private opinion endowed with public

[20] *The Federalist*, p. 59. Madison's definition of faction might also serve as a definition of the modern political party wedded to electoral victory and the "articulation and aggregation of interests": "By a faction I understand a number of citizens, whether amounting to a majority or a minority of the whole, who are united and actuated by some common impulse of passion, or of interest, adverse to the rights of other citizens, or to the permanent and aggregate interests of the community." Ibid., p. 54.

power; in the absence of civic education and a politically experienced citizenry, the public can only be a mouthpiece for those best able, with image, media access, money, or demagoguery, to buy it. In Burke's phrase, what cannot be accomplished openly will be achieved by "insidious art, and perverse industry, and gross misrepresentation."[21] This is no brief against democracy, no cynical censure of the incapacities of the people. It is only a precise portrait of what happens when a disfranchised public in a representative democracy is given the illusion of power during periods of popular reform.

The overall effect is one in which the checking of elite leadership occasions only divisiveness and interest conflict, no true democratization. In his devastating diagnosis of the maladies of what he called four-party government, James MacGregor Burns noted how

> American leaders have had to gain the concurrence not simply of a majority of the voters, but of majorities of different sets of voters organized around leaders in mutually checking and foot-dragging sectors of government. The price of this radical version of checks and balances has been enfeebled policy.[22]

In the end, bridling our leaders does not get us more democracy, just less leadership. It does not make for better citizenship; it only makes for worse government.

The particular reforms initiated by crusading progressives within the Democratic party in 1968 and 1972 (detailed by other authors in this volume) were intended to enhance party democracy and secure the control of the public over the representative institutions purporting to serve them. Presidential nominating procedures received particular attention: state delegations to nominating conventions were made more representative through the abolition of unit rule and the widening of the candidate pool; proportional representation was widely discussed as a device of party reform (one is reminded of John Stuart Mill's devotion to the Hare system of proportional representation in his *Representative Government*), and the state primary system was given major impetus in preference to the old elite-controlled nominating convention at the state level. Issues, not leadership, were brought center stage; personalities and platforms rather than political acumen and experience were given star billing.

Yet, for all this, there seems to be broad, bipartisan, cross-sectional consensus on the failure of the reforms—whatever else they might

---

21 *Selected Writings*, p. 146.

22 *Deadlock*, p. 324.

have done or undone—to enhance democracy. Centrifugal forces, to be sure, did and do counter the elitist disposition of party leadership and efficient government, but paralysis rather than participation seems the most frequent outcome. Representative government, while perhaps at least partially cyclic in its movement from elite to mass and back again, seems neither in its centralizing nor in its fragmenting tendencies to serve the interests of community, citizenship, or self-government, and is thus, with respect to real democracy, ineluctably parabolic in its evolution, just as Michels claimed. Moreover, political parties, though designed to mediate authority and citizenry in a "compound" and "extended" republic (Madison), in fact turn out to be among the least satisfactory mediating institutions known to polity or society.

None of this should give much solace to the elitist critics of party reform and popular government. To the extent such critics are not merely venting their hostility to democracy *tout court,* they are generally doing little more than completing the antidemocratic logic of the elite-mass-elite cycle. Institutional authority is preferred to popular authority because it is insulated from popular opinion. Elite leadership is preferred to mass leadership because it promises to be less demagogic and more professional and efficient. State conventions are preferred to primaries for presidential nominations because they maintain traditional political elites in place. At bottom is the deeply cynical view of the people as mass, of voters as—in James Q. Wilson's appalling phrase—"amateur democrats" whose activity is the greatest single threat to efficient republican government.[23] With this view and its attendant appeal to old-fashioned elitist politics, we simply come full circle in the Michels syndrome portrayed above, with all the contradictions of centripetal party elements reemerging.

Centripetal and centrifugal tendencies built into the representative system do then appear to precipitate polar elite/mass forces that are destabilizing to government and subversive of democracy. The party government compromise does not mediate efficient authority and popular sovereignty; it merely embodies and exacerbates their defining incompatibility.

The Strong Theory of Democracy and the Making of Citizens

If the foregoing analysis is correct, the crisis of party is a crisis of democracy and the crisis of democracy is a crisis of theory as well as practice. That is to say, it suggests a fundamental incoherence in

[23] *The Amateur Democrat* (Chicago: University of Chicago Press, 1962). The phrase has been used more recently by neoconservative critics of democracy.

the theory of representative democracy—or as I shall call it here, the "thin" theory of democracy. Representative democracy is a thin theory of democracy because it holds democratic values only provisionally: they are prudential, conditional, or instrumental with respect to other ends (negative freedom, rights, private property, and so forth) that are themselves individualistic and privatistic. No firm belief in the intrinsic worth of citizenship, participation, public goods, community, and self-government can be expected to be nourished by this instrumentalism. Representative democracy can thus never really be too far from Ambrose Bierce's cynical formulation of politics as "the conduct of public affairs for private advantage"; it must always be more concerned to promote individual liberty than to secure public justice, to advance interests (whether mass or elite) than to discover public goods, to keep individuals safely apart (government as the adjudication of conflicting interests through party representation) than to bring them fruitfully together (government as the pursuit of community goods through communal self-government). It is a democracy that defines the crucial ingredient of popular sovereignty as control rather than participation—thus Robert Dahl's well-known construction of democracy as "at a minimum . . . concerned with processes by which ordinary citizens exert a relatively high degree of control over leaders,"[24] or David Easton's "a political system in which power is so distributed that control over the authoritative allocation of values lies in the hands of the mass of the people."[25]

Yet Reinhold Niebuhr lamented many years ago that democracy must have "a more compelling justification and requires a more realistic vindication than is given it by the liberal culture with which it has been associated in modern history."[26] It seems apparent that representative democracy in both its elite and mass party variations has not and will not provide that justification. The apathy and alienation and anomie that are found on the underbelly of America's vaunted freedoms, the rootlessness and anonymity that makes normal familial, kinship, and neighborly relations so problematic, the privatizing, interest-balancing approach characteristic of putatively "public" policy making, the sapping materialism of the nation's economic successes as well as the devastation occasioned by its economic failures, and the paralysis of both presidential and congressional government in the

[24] *A Preface to Democratic Theory* (Chicago: University of Chicago Press, 1956), p. 3.

[25] *Political Systems* (New York: Alfred A. Knopf, 1953), p. 222.

[26] *The Children of Light and the Children of Darkness* (New York: Scribner's, 1944), pp. 5-6.

face of a party system that seems equally incapable of mobilizing and engaging citizens or creating and motivating effective leaders all point to the inadequacy of the thin theory of democracy and its supporting representative institutions. Its provisionality ultimately makes representative government a citizen-corroding, community-denying instrument of elite and mass interests. It can know no form of citizenship other than the sometime voter and the hungry client, and can achieve no public purpose other than the self-interested trade-off and the prudent bargain.

Representative democracy is thus always weak democracy and can never yield the pleasures of participation or the fellowship of fraternity, the individual strength of community membership or the mutuality of public goods, and, perhaps most essential, can never comprehend that all-too-human interdependency that underlies all political life.

The "strong" theory of democracy, as I would like to call it,[27] takes Rousseau as its mentor, and concurs with John Dewey in understanding democracy not as "an alternate to other principles of associated life [but as] the idea of community life itself. . . . [It is] a name for a life of free and enriching communion."[28] It begins with the idea that there can be no "amateurs" in politics because there can be no professionals, and insists that sovereignty can neither be alienated nor represented without eventually destroying the autonomy of the individual or people represented.

Representative democracy, as weak democracy, tends to instruct women and men in their rights and offers them tools for selecting and controlling the elites who govern them; strong democracy instructs them in their obligations (inextricably bound up with rights) and teaches them how to govern themselves. Where weak democracy is marked exclusively by the language of right, interest, power, privacy, contract, and representation, strong democracy employs a language of citizenship, community, fraternity, responsibility, obligation, and self-realization as well—not to the exclusion of the first set of terms, but to ground them in the actual conditions of interdependency and sociability that constitute the real social and economic environment of politics.

Michael Oakeshott may think he is portraying only conservative politics when he depicts the political condition as that of sailors on

---

[27] "The Strong Theory of Democracy: A Communitarian Challenge to Liberalism," manuscript.

[28] *The Public and Its Problems* (Chicago: Swallow Press, 1954; reprint of 1924 ed.), p. 148.

a "boundless and bottomless sea [where] there is neither harbour nor shelter nor floor for anchorage, neither starting-place nor appointed destination [and where] the enterprise is to keep afloat on an even keel";[29] but he is also portraying a politics that *is* an end rather than one that only *has* ends, a politics where the communal spirit kindled by sailing is as important as potential communal destinations—one where, most importantly, such destinations as are discovered or invented represent not the private interests of a manipulating elite or the private passions of a manipulated mass but the deliberate common will of a community of active citizens.

Despite the several virtues of the strong theory of democracy and the many deficiencies of thin or representative democracy, the strong theory remains an ideal which even in the Founders' era could be dismissed as irrelevant (if not insidious) in the context of a burgeoning continental republic at once both extended and compound. What possible bearing can it have on the pressing exigencies of party government in America today? Were the Founders not finally deeply wise (as Edward C. Banfield insists in this volume and throughout his corpus) in their refusal to base government on direct participation by a people which, if not always as hungry as Hamilton's Beast, was nonetheless never for its own good to be trusted with rulership?

Certainly there seems to be wide consensus among both neo-Burkean conservatives like Robert Nisbet and Samuel Huntington and neo-Marxist radicals like Peter Bachrach[30] that the people, or that false consciousness that parades itself in the people's proletarian garb, are not to be trusted. Radicals fear that ordinary women and men, if given the chance, will cripple government with narrow-minded, unthinking conservatism of the kind exhibited in California's Proposition 13, or will repeal the Bill of Rights in the name of law and order, or will precipitate other outrages equally offensive to (radical)

---

[29] *Rationalism in Politics* (New York: Basic Books, 1962), p. 127.

[30] See Peter Bachrach, Testimony before the Subcommittee on the Constitution of the Committee on the Judiciary on S. J. Res. 67, 95th Cong., 1st sess., Dec. 13-14, 1977.

It is particularly disheartening to see critics of elitism who spring from the popular Left join the outcry against such populist institutions as the referendum in America. Once again, however, Michels perceived the danger seventy-five years ago when he wrote:

> Where party life is concerned, the socialists for the most part reject . . . practical applications of democracy, using against them conservative arguments such as we are otherwise accustomed to hear only from the opponents of socialism. In articles written by socialist leaders it is ironically asked whether it would be a good thing to hand over the leadership of the party to the ignorant masses simply for love of an abstract democratic principle. (*Political Parties*, p. 336.)

good sense. Conservatives fear that the same women and men, if given the chance, will form into clamoring special interest groups that are already overrepresented in the system and force government into imprudent expenditures for conservation and social welfare or demand nefarious cutbacks in defense spending, or precipitate other outrages equally offensive to (conservative) good sense. This kind of scapegoating at the people's expense is typical of the long campaign representative democracy's advocates have waged against participatory democracy.

The strategy is elementary but not ineffective: give the people all the insignia but none of the tools of citizenship and accuse them of incompetence; throw referenda at them without providing civic education or insulation from money and media and then pillory them for their ill-judgment; inundate them with problem issues the "experts" have not been able to solve (busing, inflation, atomic energy, right-to-work legislation) and then carp at their uncertainty or indecisiveness or simple-mindedness in muddling through to a position.

Yet voters do not become citizens overnight any more than clients become autonomous self-governors in the course of a day. Representative government has had two hundred years in which to commit a thousand errors; direct popular government is rarely given more than a single chance. Certainly there is neither hope for nor point in trying to "convert" from representative to direct democracy or to substitute at the wave of a hand or the waiver of a constitution some strange breed of federalized participatory assembly rule for two-party government. There is more than enough room for a shift of emphasis, however—away from party realignment and electoral reform and toward institutional modification favorable to greater public participation not in the selection of governors but in governing itself. These institutions, nourished by the strong theory of democracy, would have as their purpose the making of citizens as well as the making of public policy, and might include experiments in common legislation and common work as well as in common deliberation and common decision making. I have discussed (in the context of America's political realities) the promise as well as the problems of such institutional changes elsewhere,[31] but I can repeat here that the objective, initially, is a change in emphasis, attitude, and spirit rather than a radical remaking of the American system of government.

[31] See my *Political Participation and the Creation of Res Publica*, Poynter Pamphlet (Bloomington, Ind.: Poynter Center, 1977), particularly pp. 13-19; see also my testimony before the Subcommittee on the Constitution of the Committee on the Judiciary on S. J. Res. 67, 95th Cong., 1st sess., Dec. 13-14, 1977.

John Stuart Mill, no friend of direct democracy though an admirer of proportional representation and a powerful believer in the necessity of civic education and a morally alive citizenry, issued a warning in *On Liberty* that has been widely overlooked by his teeming liberal fans:

> The mischief begins when, instead of calling forth the activity and powers of individuals and bodies, [a government] substitutes its own activity for theirs; when, instead of informing, advising, and, upon occasion, denouncing, it makes them work in fetters, or bids them stand aside and does their work instead of them. The worth of a State, in the long run, is the worth of the individuals composing it; and a State which postpones the interests of *their* mental expansion and elevation to a little more of administrative skill . . . in the details of business; a State which dwarfs its men, in order that they may be more docile instruments in its hands even for beneficial purposes—will find that with small men no great thing can really be accomplished; and that the perfection of machinery to which it has sacrificed everything will in the end avail it nothing, for want of the vital power which, in order that the machine might work more smoothly, it has preferred to banish.[32]

In America, the "vital power" has been banished by party government; what is worse, the machine refuses to run smoothly for all that! The system has certainly provided that "degree of circumspection and distrust" of which Madison, in *Federalist* Number 55, deemed mankind's "depravity" worthy; but Madison suggested in the same passage that there were also "other qualities in human nature which justify a certain portion of esteem and confidence,"[33] and those have been barely recognized let alone honored and institutionalized in the American party system. Consequently, it may indeed be true that Americans are today *small* women and men incapable of any great thing. Still, great things are required of our nation in the coming years—not least among them, survival as a democracy—and it seems clear enough that if those things are to be achieved, voters and clients will have to become, if not great women and men, at least active, participating citizens in the governance of our public life.

---

[32] (London: Everyman's Library, n.d.), p. 170.

[33] *The Federalist*, p. 365.

4

The News Media as an Alternative to Party in the Presidential Selection Process

Nelson W. Polsby

The Decline of Parties

Because presidential nominations take place only quadrennially, historical change seems to proceed not in gradual modulations, like a strip of moving picture film, but in a sharply discontinuous series of snapshots. In 1952, after Estes Kefauver entered the New Hampshire Democratic primary, Harry Truman, who had not yet declared himself out of the race, pronounced primary elections "eyewash."[1] In those days, even when there were real delegates at stake rather than a mere beauty contest, primary elections were at best an aid to the calculations of party leaders. They provided data—the significance of which was debatable and debated—about the capacity of those presidential aspirants willing to subject themselves to this sort of test to mobilize support among restricted but indubitably mass electorates. When leaders met to pick a nominee, recent hard information about the popularity of various candidates could be useful, though not necessarily dispositive, in influencing the outcome.[2] In 1948 Harold Stassen had debated Thomas E. Dewey in Oregon, and the results of that state's primary had knocked Stassen out of contention.[3] In 1952 Dwight Eisenhower's overwhelming write-in vote in Minnesota must

---

[1] See Paul T. David, Malcolm Moos, and Ralph M. Goldman, *Presidential Nominating Politics in 1952*, vol. 2 (Baltimore: Johns Hopkins University Press, 1954) p. 44.

[2] My codification of textbook descriptions of the process is contained in "Decision-making at the National Party Conventions," *Western Political Quarterly*, vol. 13 (September 1960), pp. 609-19.

[3] See Jules Abels, *Out of the Jaws of Victory* (New York: Henry Holt, 1959), pp. 57ff.; and Irwin Ross, *The Loneliest Campaign* (New York: New American Library, 1968), pp. 47-53.

have turned away from Senator Robert Taft more than a few delegates who wanted a winner more than they wanted their favorite Republican.[4]

The next snapshot is dated 1960. Taking advantage of a political division within the Democratic party of Ohio, candidate John F. Kennedy thwarted Governor Mike DiSalle's efforts to bring an uncommitted delegation to the national convention. Because public opinion polls suggested that Kennedy could beat any favorite son in the primary, DiSalle changed his plans and ran as the head of a Kennedy delegation, thereby forestalling a challenge from the Cleveland faction of the party.[5] By 1960, entering and winning primaries was a method for forcing political leaders—no matter what their private inclinations—to take a candidate seriously. Kennedy in 1960 was no more beloved among Senate Democrats than was Kefauver in 1952, but in a fragmented field, with no incumbent president to orchestrate an opposition, primary victories meant more. Consequently, also, candidate initiatives meant more and party leaders correspondingly less in the overall process of choosing.

It is useful to keep these snapshots in mind as we consider the revolution of 1968. They suggest that longer term forces were at work pressing the presidential selection process in the direction it suddenly lurched in that busy and dreadful year. The key historical events of 1968, from the perspective of party politics, were the disorderly withdrawal of Lyndon Johnson, the assassination of Robert Kennedy, and the election of Richard Nixon.[6]

Johnson withdrew after Eugene McCarthy's surprisingly good showing in the New Hampshire primary. He maintained ever after that had he remained in the race, he would have been renominated

---

[4] David, Moos, and Goldman, *Nominating Politics*, vol. 4, pp. 172-73.

[5] Aaron Wildavsky, "What Can I Do? Ohio Delegates View the Democratic Convention," in *Inside Politics: The National Convention, 1960*, ed. Paul Tillett (Dobbs Ferry, N.Y.: Oceana, 1962), pp. 112-31.

[6] Most narrative accounts of this election are unsatisfactory because of their fixation on Eugene McCarthy and his reformers and on Robert Kennedy and his entourage, to the exclusion of what was going on in the bulk of the Democratic party. Being mesmerized by Kennedys is an acknowledged flaw in Theodore White's books, as John A. Garraty's review of White's autobiography, *In Search of History*, stresses. *American Historical Review*, vol. 84 (June 1979), pp. 869-70. See, however, *The Making of the President 1968* (New York: Atheneum, 1969). Other accounts displaying similar difficulties include two English productions: David English, *Divided They Stand* (London: Michael Joseph, 1969); and Lewis Chester, Godfrey Hodgson, and Bruce Page, *An American Melodrama* (New York: Viking, 1969). To find out much of anything about what was going on in the camp of the actual Democratic nominee, it is necessary to read Hubert Humphrey, *The Education of a Public Man* (Garden City, N.Y.: Doubleday, 1976). One hopes that in due course this memoir will be supplemented by more extensive materials.

and reelected, and there is reason to think he was right. Johnson's control over the national convention in 1968, even though he was a lame duck, suggests that he could have been embarrassed but not defeated, at least within the party. However, his need to maintain an iron grip over the party hurt his political heir greatly: the full consequences of the Democratic party's disarray fell upon Hubert Humphrey.

Soon after Johnson withdrew in March 1968, the elites of the party split into three camps. McCarthy led a group who believed that a runaway presidency was a major cause of continued American participation in the Vietnam war and that a way to withdraw from the war was to curb the presidency. Robert Kennedy, after an earlier alliance with this group, led an influential fraction of the Democratic elite who favored withdrawal from the war, but who did not think it was necessary to sacrifice the presidency to accomplish this end. Humphrey was left with that fraction of the elite that stood behind the president's conduct of the war as a part of its support for the presidency.

Humphrey's best—perhaps his only—strategy for winning the 1968 election was straightforward. He was compelled by Johnson's sudden withdrawal to fight for the nomination as the candidate of the Johnson wing of the party. Then he had to make his peace—along with concessions on Vietnam more or less reflecting his own privately held views—with the Kennedy wing. McCarthy had no real chance of winning the nomination. Robert Kennedy's ability to dislodge allegedly "soft" Humphrey delegates in the South and in the labor movement depended upon a massive show of popularity in the California primary—a result that did not materialize.[7] The Kennedy assassination aborted the process of intraparty reconciliation. Instead of having to deal with the manageable disaffections of Eugene McCarthy and his followers, Humphrey was faced with the grief-stricken, angry intransigence of a far more sizable fraction of the Democratic elite.

[7] Kennedy won 46 percent of the vote in California, McCarthy 42 percent. Analyses contrary to mine are legion and constitute a lasting tribute to the excellent relations of the Kennedy family with the press. See, e.g., David Halberstam's *The Unfinished Odyssey of Robert Kennedy* (New York: Random House, 1968), p. 214, a work amply displaying symptoms for which this same author's *The Best and the Brightest* (New York: Random House, 1969) is supposed to be the cure; and Jack Newfield's, *Robert Kennedy: A Memoir* (New York: Bantam, 1970). Other interpretations of the California primary include Richard Scammon and Ben Wattenberg, *The Real Majority* (New York: Coward, McCann, 1970), pp. 135-40; Chester, Hodgson, and Page, *Melodrama*, p. 357; and Arthur Herzog, *McCarthy for President* (New York: Viking, 1969), p. 173.

This was the historical context of the sweeping recommendations for party reform that came out of the 1968 convention and its creature, the McGovern-Fraser Commission. Humphrey, congenitally hospitable to the principle of institutional reform in any event, was eager to placate alienated branches of the party and achieve a semblance of unity against the Republicans. Out of Humphrey's eagerness and the desire of the Kennedy and McCarthy groups in part for revenge and in part for remedies for their powerlessness at the 1968 convention, came the reforms of the Democratic party. These reforms, when combined with changes in federal law, constituted a fundamental reshaping of the nomination process and of the role of party within that process.

The election of Richard Nixon in 1968 had two consequences for the future of party reform. First, it deprived the Democratic party at a critical juncture of an incumbent president who could have taken a hand in the management of the reform process in the interests of the traditionally organized state parties and their allies—chiefly the AFL-CIO—among Democratic coalition interest groups. As a consequence, the McGovern-Fraser Commission was managed very much by the party's left—by representatives of volunteer and amateur-dominated rather than traditionally organized state parties and by staff members from the dissident wings of the party.[8] President Nixon's second contribution came at the end of his first term: Watergate gave an impetus to laws providing for federally financed political campaigns.

A final snapshot: In the election of 1976, the first delegates of the year were selected in January by a state convention in Iowa. Thirty-seven percent of those selected were "uncommitted." Next in line was Jimmy Carter, with 28 percent; other Democratic hopefuls strung along with smaller percentages.[9] Roger Mudd of CBS named Carter the "clear winner." In New Hampshire, where Carter got 30 percent of the vote, Walter Cronkite spoke of his "commanding head

[8] One example of "management": it was decided that members of the McGovern Commission could not send substitutes to meetings. This, among other things, alienated I. W. Abel, president of the United Steel Workers and a traditionalist within the party. While Abel could not send his representative, the United Auto Workers, a more liberal union, had their Washington representative, William Dodds, appointed directly to the commission, thus avoiding Abel's problem. See Byron E. Shafer, "The Party Reformed," Ph.D. dissertation, University of California, Berkeley, 1979, which documents this and numerous other examples of the exercise of managerial options by the commission.

[9] The percentages were: uncommitted 37.0; Carter 27.6; Bayh 13.1; Harris 9.9; Udall 5.9; and Shriver 3.3.

start."[10] And so it proved: by the time Carter had won a little over one-third of the delegates to the national convention, the overwhelming consensus was that a "magic number" had been reached, and such fence-sitting notables as Chicago Mayor Richard J. Daley came out for Carter.[11] The nomination process was over, well in advance of the national convention. In a scant two and a half decades, it was the national convention that had become "eyewash."

The Impact of Party Rules Changes

The chief consequence of the decision by the Democratic national committee to adopt the McGovern-Fraser Commission's "guidelines" was to convince a sizable number of state party leaders that they could best avoid a challenge to their delegates to the 1972 national convention by shifting to a primary election process. Thus the presidential selection process in the Democratic party moved from a system that mixed primary elections with state conventions—with party elites still dominating the process—to a system in which delegate selection was dominated by the choices of primary electorates.[12] Further incentives were extended to prospective candidates by the federal law providing matching funds for the primary election races of major party candidates who could raise modest amounts of money ($5,000 in donations of $250 or less) in twenty states.[13] The unit rule was outlawed in the Democratic party, giving even more incentives to contestants, since the possibility existed that even a small effort might reap a reward in delegates.

[10] See Paul Weaver, "Captives of Melodrama," *New York Times Magazine*, August 29, 1976, p. 6. This and other discussions of the media in politics are ably summarized in Max M. Kampelman, "The Power of the Press: A Problem for Our Democracy," *Policy Review*, vol. 6 (Fall 1978), pp. 7-39.

[11] On June 8, 1976, when Carter had 38 percent of the delegates then allocated, Mayor Daley said, "This man, Carter, has fought in every primary, and if he wins in Ohio, he'll walk in under his own power." See Jules Witcover, *Marathon* (New York: Viking, 1977), p. 349. Carter won in Ohio but on the same day lost in New Jersey and California. The final primary elections of June 9 gave Carter 39 percent of the total delegates. The remaining 61 percent were widely spread, including an uncommitted 18 percent. See Donald R. Matthews, "Winnowing," in *Race for the Presidency*, ed. J. D. Barber (Englewood Cliffs, N.J.: Prentice-Hall, 1978), p. 72, table 3.

[12] The number of primaries went from fifteen in 1968 (selecting 40 percent of the delegates) to thirty in 1976, selecting 76 percent. The figures are roughly the same for Republicans. See Austin Ranney, *Curing the Mischiefs of Faction* (Berkeley: University of California Press, 1975), esp. p. 206, for analysis of these and other party reforms in historical perspective.

[13] By February 1979, George Bush, as an unannounced but possible candidate, had already qualified for federal matching funds for his race for the 1980 Republican nomination. Two announced candidates, John Connally and Philip Crane, had also qualified. This fortifies my view that the threshold for participation is not onerously high.

These three major changes in the rules of the game drastically shifted the structure of incentives toward direct initiatives by candidates and the cultivation by candidates of mass electorates. The gate-keeping functions of party leaders and party organizations were permitted to atrophy. Under these rules, candidates, not party leaders, would dominate the presidential selection process from 1968 onward. Candidate enthusiasts, not state party loyalists, would make up the battalions of delegates to national party conventions.

The principal mechanisms through which candidates and their enthusiasts exercise their power are the mass media of news dissemination. A major effect of the reforms and legal changes identified above has been to supplant internal communication within the major parties with various forms of public communication. Party fund-raising, for example, once a significant device for promoting social contact among donors and politicians, has been replaced in the presidential nomination campaign by low-priced mass meetings and rallies, on the model of a rock concert, and, even more importantly, by mail solicitations. The targets of mail solicitations and primary electorates are both more responsive to mass publicity than anything else. Thus the fundamental effect of changes in the rules of the game has been to weaken the influence of parties and party elites on presidential nominations and to strengthen elites who have access to the devices and the channels of mass publicity: public relations and media technicians who work for the various candidates, rock stars and movie "personalities,"[14] and more significantly, the professional journalists (this includes news broadcast producers and newspaper publishers) whose direct access to the news media gives them influence over the content of the national news diet.

It is certainly true, as advocates of these changes have argued, that participation in the nomination process has been greatly expanded as a result. Hundreds of thousands now participate in the delegate selection process, once the province of perhaps no more than a few thousand party stalwarts. The process has also been transformed from an exercise in elite persuasion to an exercise in mass persuasion.

[14] See Joel Kotkin and Paul Grabowicz, "The New Star Trek: Cashing in on Politics," *Washington Post Outlook*, February 25, 1979. "Prominent among the emerging powers is a strange new breed of Hollywood movie stars and rock singers—not issue advocates of the Robert Redford, Shirley MacLaine, or Marlon Brando variety, but a group whose political talent is simply to raise more campaign cash in a night than others might have in a year. Indeed, the new group fittingly cares far more about personalities than about issues, if it thinks about issues at all."

The Workways of Media Elites

Some observers have been slower than others to grasp the consequences of these changes. Some who worked for the changes have voiced misgivings, suggesting that not all consequences of party reform were anticipated.[15] By now, however, only a few diehards fail to concede that the national parties are in serious trouble.[16] To say that parties are in trouble is to say little more than that party elites have lost influence over the central activities of parties. The diminution of party loyalty in the electorate and the decline of turnout in presidential elections, insofar as they are bona fide phenomena of contemporary American politics, are (1) incremental and not massive changes and (2) may well be the *results* of changes at the elite level rather than, as reformers frequently argue, reasons for these changes.[17]

[15] E.g., Ranney, *Curing the Mischiefs*, pp. 191, 207-9.

[16] An example of how this sort of trouble proliferates: Many observers claim that there has been a great burgeoning in the influence of so-called single-issue interest groups. I think what they are witnessing is not the proliferation of single-issue interests, which have always existed and attempted to influence the political process, but rather a precipitous decline in the capacity of party elites to resist, channel, or accommodate such demands short of ceding extraordinary influence over the nomination process to them.

[17] The best single summary I have seen on the turnout question is Richard Brody, "The Puzzle of Political Participation in America," in *The New American Political System*, ed. Anthony King (Washington, D.C.: American Enterprise Institute, 1978), pp. 287-324. A recent comprehensive analysis on the "independent voter" phenomenon is a manuscript shortly to be published by the American Enterprise Institute by Raymond E. Wolfinger and associates. Some salient figures (from Michigan surveys in the indicated years) show not much increase in independent voting over a twenty-year span, as indicated in the accompanying table.

Independent Voters, 1956–1976

Election Year	*% Defected from Party Identification in Voting*		*% Self-Identified as Independent and "Leaning" Independent*
	Presidential Election	House Election	
1956	15	9	9
1958	—	11	—
1960	13	12	8
1962	—	12	—
1964	15	15	5
1966	—	16	—
1968	23	19	9
1970	—	16	—
1972	25	17	8
1974	—	18	—
1976	15	19	11

Source: Raymond E. Wolfinger, Martin Shapiro, and Fred Greenstein, *Dynamics of American Politics*, 2d ed. (Englewood Cliffs, N.J.: Prentice-Hall, 1980), chap. 8.

If party elites are losing influence in the American system of presidential nomination to media elites, then it seems sensible to inquire about the performance we can expect from media elites in this role. This requires knowledge of the workways of the news media, which have already been carefully studied.[18] Those workways may be reduced to two organizational imperatives: professionalism and competitiveness.

Professionalism demands that news media elites establish their own account of day-to-day reality, independent of that propounded by the politicians whom they cover. It should come as no surprise that there are frequent disagreements between the two about the proper interpretation of reality. News media professionals regard these disagreements as an earnest of their own professionalism. Politicians occasionally take the view that news people are attempting to create an "adversary culture" and are purveyors of radical chic.[19] My view is that the news media can be considered chic, but not necessarily radical. That is, news people readily absorb the thinking of people like themselves—increasingly the educated and articulate segments of the population—and tend to act as transmitters and amplifiers of such ideas, especially when they are different from and even antagonistic to what governments are saying, because this helps to warrant the news media elite's independent professionalism.

Competitiveness acts in three ways to modify this picture, providing incentives for compression, for impact, and for convergence. Compression is a response to the severe time constraints that prevent news media managers from dealing with the vast bulk of the material presented to them by any but the most ritualized means. Competitiveness presses journalists to get a story first and report it quickly—the old scoop mentality. There is simply no time, except in rare circumstances, for reporters or editors to mull over what is going on, or for second thoughts to have an impact on the way most stories are reported or played. Thus news stories tend to become highly stereotyped in the ways in which they are perceived by media professionals, who shape them into standardized dramatic structures. As one ex-

---

[18] The locus classicus is Bernard C. Cohen, *The Press and Foreign Policy* (Princeton: Princeton University Press, 1963). Further explorations of the same themes can be found in a series of Harvard doctoral dissertations, e.g., Edward Jay Epstein, *News from Nowhere* (New York: Random House, 1973); Leon Segal, *Reporters and Officials* (Lexington, Mass.: D. C. Heath, 1973); Paul Weaver, "The Metropolitan Newspaper as a Political Institution," 1969; Paul Weaver, "How the *Times* is Slanted Down the Middle," *New York*, July 1, 1968, pp. 32-36.

[19] See, e.g., Daniel Patrick Moynihan, *Coping* (New York: Random House, 1973), pp. 318-20.

ample, Paul Weaver has described the horse-race scenario of the presidential primaries, and Thomas Patterson has taken the trouble to document the way this scenario dominated the coverage of the 1976 preconvention campaign.[20]

Competitiveness also encourages attempts to maximize impact, both on readers/viewers and on political actors. A famous newsman once remarked to me that there were always more deaths on the UPI ticker's first account of any disaster—a harmless attempt, it was well understood, by the second-place wire service to nudge the better established AP's story out of as many papers as possible.[21] Impact on political actors increases the credibility of a news organization with its customers and hence helps it competitively. American television viewers are used to having the most significant question at any presidential press conference being asked by the CBS reporter, according to CBS news, and so forth. Modern presidents must be prepared to declare the same war three separate times, once for each network, if they intend to do so in response to a press conference question.

To be convincing purveyors of reality, and if possible more convincing than the competition, journalists must get as close as they can to the sources of events. This means access to political leaders, to whom they give publicity as a quid pro quo for the proximity that lends verisimilitude to their accounts.[22] Competitiveness thus entails snuggling up to news sources, and works at cross-purposes with the imperative of professionalism to maintain independence. The tensions, both institutional and personal, that result from this contradictory set of demands are endless.

One might think that competition would lead to product differentiation, but this depends upon marketing strategies. On the whole it does not work that way among the most important national news organizations.[23] The marketing strategy of the major suppliers of

[20] Weaver, "Captives of Melodrama"; Patterson, "Press Coverage and Candidate Success in Presidential Primaries: The 1976 Democratic Race," paper delivered at the Annual Meeting of The American Political Science Association, Washington, D.C., 1977.

[21] See Daniel Machalba, "UPI Struggles As It Loses Ground to AP, Other News Services," *Wall Street Journal*, July 11, 1979, pp. 1, 37.

[22] Here is a slightly comic example of the process at work: "The United States finds it hard to understand why King Hussein . . . joined the outcry against Camp David. . . . But there are reasons for the policy from the Jordanian viewpoint. They were explained to me by Hussein's articulate brother, Crown Prince Hassan—the King is abroad—and by high officials." Anthony Lewis, "At Home Abroad: When Friends Fall Out," *New York Times*, April 16, 1979, p. A17.

[23] For our purposes there are the three networks, the two wire services, the two big news magazines, and the handful of big newspapers owning their own national syndication services, principally the *New York Times* and the *Washington Post*–

news—appealing to the fat part of the market rather than to specialists—entails a systematic suppression of detail and a search for instantaneous coherence, however spurious. This causes reporters and editors alike to monitor and, tacitly or explicitly, to collude with the competition. Nobody who intends to supply the masses with their daily ration of news can afford to be out on a limb too often, peddling what may come to be viewed as an idiosyncratic version of reality. Since the realities for a newspaper are mostly social and political realities, they depend on consensual definitions of the situation, and most news organizations most of the time willingly participate in that consensus, sometimes to the advantage of undeserving politicians, sometimes to their equally unmerited disadvantage.

I believe this analysis accounts for most if not all the evils of the press as interpreted by critics as diverse as Spiro Agnew and Daniel Patrick Moynihan, and does so without recourse to imputations of bad faith, ugly motives, or malicious intent. A fair number of newsmen have these—they are not clustered at one end of the political spectrum, by the way—and do let them show in their work, but these factors simply do not begin to account for what is going on. Rather, the product we see is the result of widely shared subcultural norms of professional conduct and of conventional mass marketing strategies under highly competitive circumstances.

Some Properties of Mass Decision Making

These workways have had a distinctive institutional impact on the presidential nominating process. Many people have noted various changes that I am about to mention. The contribution of this discussion is to characterize these changes as parts of an underlying transformation of the nomination process from an elite to a mass phenomenon. Advocates of this transformation have appealed to the neutral principle of political equality: far more people now participate in the process than was true before 1968. This has been accomplished, however, at the cost of deliberation. Mass politics entails highly stylized interactions among political actors. Those at the focus of mass attention do a very high proportion of the stimulating in the system and retain most of the options for action. Mass participants typically can make their views known by voting—or conceivably by

Los Angeles Times. Readers will recognize that differentiated marketing strategies are at work for otherwise important news organizations like the *Wall Street Journal* and *U.S. News and World Report,* for whom deductions from the axiom of competitiveness must be suitably modified.

letter-writing, where letters for and against various options are weighed rather than read.[24]

Interactive decision making distributes more widely the entitlement to influence the agenda of decision makers than noninteractive, mass, "participatory" decision making.[25] It facilitates processes of deliberation, which entail such activities as varying the sequence in which options are considered, testing different paired comparisons, investigating the structures of participants' preferences for such characteristics as the identities of second and third choices, intensities of preferences, strongly held anathemas, transitivities and intransitivities, and so on. None of this is easy and much of it is impossible in mass decision-making processes.

Perhaps the single most significant consequence of the transformation of a set of decisions from deliberative to nondeliberative modes is the vast increase in the likelihood that eventual choices will be artifacts of formal properties of the choice process rather than reflective of distributions of opinions within the appropriate population. A fair number of theorists take the view that the act of choosing is a valid method of discovering opinions. It is unclear to me whether all methods are held to be equally valid. But if we for the moment accept that opinions can be discovered independently of the choice processes that enact them into law or embody them institutionally, it is possible to speak of decision-making processes that are better and worse at taking account of opinions in a given population.

Some of the formal properties of mass, nondeliberative decision making that seem to me highly consequential for presidential nominations are the following:

1. *The sequence of choices.* Early choices greatly color the way later alternatives are perceived. The news media give enormous coverage to, and prematurely force coherence upon the results of, the earliest primaries and state conventions. The strategic options for

[24] An example of this sort of citizen participation appears in a recent account of the Edward R. Murrow television broadcast criticizing Senator Joseph McCarthy: "CBS said it was the greatest spontaneous response in the history of broadcasting: 12,348 telephone calls and telegrams in the first few hours. According to the network, 11,567 of these supported Murrow. (Today the CBS vaults contain 22 boxes, each containing between 750 and 1000 communications. Eighteen are marked 'Favorable' and the remaining four, 'Unfavorable')." Joseph Wershba, "Murrow vs. McCarthy: See it Now," *New York Times Magazine*, March 4, 1979, p. 37. In a mass situation, those citizens who composed thoughtful letters might just as well have sent in ballots check-marked "favorable" or "unfavorable."

[25] The problems of interaction under conditions of widespread participation are discussed in Robert A. Dahl and Edward Tufte, *Size and Democracy* (Stanford: Stanford University Press, 1973), esp. pp. 66-88.

political leaders, candidates, and party influentials alike are increasingly foreclosed by the publicity blitz of the early primaries, the competitive pressure for reaction stories. The New Hampshire primary has been blown all out of proportion to the number of delegates picked there. As Michael Robinson put it, "In proportionate terms, each Democratic vote in New Hampshire received 170 times as much network news time as each Democratic vote in New York. Media reality —television reality—implied that a victory in New Hampshire totally overwhelmed a victory in New York."[26]

2. *The number of alternatives on the ballot (especially where only first choices are counted).* If Kenneth Arrow had advised Henry Jackson to get into the 1976 New Hampshire primary the results of the entire race might have been changed. The "liberal" vote split four ways, and Jimmy Carter came out ahead by differentiating his appeal as a relatively conservative candidate rather than consolidating support from a wide base. As we all know, this is how Lyndon Johnson won his first congressional free-for-all primary. Getting a majority does not matter under the rules most commonly in use to cope with large flocks of candidates. Being up there in a rank order—first or in the top two—matters much more. The preferred strategy encourages factionalism (bring out your own voters) and discourages coalition building (making deals to reach a majority).[27]

3. *The number of elections held simultaneously.* The mass media cannot digest complex results. Winning everywhere is perfectly acceptable, but anything short of that gives the media indigestion and is less advantageous than winning on a day when there is only one primary election.

4. *Balloting systems.* By the rules, only first choices are counted. Second choices are the preemptive invention of the media. Thus a vote for Eugene McCarthy in the 1968 New Hampshire primary was uniformly assumed to embody a second choice for Robert Kennedy. Much later it was discovered that large numbers of Vietnam hawks

---

[26] "TV's Newest Program: 'The Presidential Nominations Game,'" *Public Opinion*, vol. 1 (May-June 1978), pp. 41-46. See also Michael J. Robinson and Karen A. McPherson, "Television News Coverage before the 1976 New Hampshire Primary: The Focus of Network Journalism," *Journal of Broadcasting*, vol. 21 (Spring 1977), pp. 177-86; Michael J. Robinson and Karen A. McPherson, "The Early Presidential Campaign on Network Television," in *Social Responsibilities of the Mass Media*, ed. A. Casebier and J. J. Casebier (Washington, D.C.: University Press of America, 1978), pp. 5-41.

[27] My elaborated thoughts on this subject are contained in "Coalition and Faction in American Politics: An Institutional View," in *Coalitions in American Politics*, ed. S. M. Lipset (San Francisco: Institute of Contemporary Affairs, 1978), pp. 103-23.

voted for McCarthy; in fact, the bulk of his support came from this source. They may well have confused him with another Midwestern senator of the same name who died in the mid-1950s.[28] We cannot be sure that Robert Kennedy would have benefited from the same misapprehension.

In any event, second choices are, in the American presidential nominating system under its new, participatory rules, the property of media elites to distribute and not of participants or voters. The rule of thumb for candidates is, it is far better to be the first choice of 30 percent of delegates in a nondeliberative system than the second choice of 90 percent. In a nondeliberative system there are no mechanisms available to consider second choices.

In all these respects, the quality of participation is sacrificed to quantity of participants. In presidential election years where for all practical purposes there is only one choice, or the party must choose between only two alternatives, the costs in deliberative capacity do not seem terribly onerous. Difficulties arise when there is a more complex set of decisions to be made, and the rules as presently constituted do give incentives for the proliferation rather than the restriction of alternatives.

Moreover, the claim that greater participation enhances the political equality of party members is seriously flawed in one important respect. This arises because of the characteristics of voters who tend to turn out in primary elections and the imposition by this population of decisions that preclude taking account of a wider constituency at later stages of decision making. These effects are so well known, and have been known for such a long time, that it is curious that they did not figure more in debates over changes in party rules. It is not merely nostalgia that invokes the memory of V. O. Key in this connection.[29] More recent research, notably by James I. Lengle, confirms for national politics the patterns noted by Key at the state level.[30]

Table 1 shows recent data (for 1976) on the representativeness of primary electorates from the Report of the Democratic party's Commission on Presidential Nomination and Party Structure (usually

[28] See Philip E. Converse, "Public Opinion and Voting Behavior," in *Handbook of Political Science*, vol. 4, ed. F. I. Greenstein and N. W. Polsby (Reading, Mass.: Addison-Wesley, 1975), p. 81.

[29] See V. O. Key, Jr., *American State Politics* (New York: Knopf, 1956), esp. chap. 5, "Participation in Primaries: The Illusion of Popular Rule."

[30] "Presidential Primaries and Representation," Ph.D. dissertation, University of California, Berkeley, 1978.

TABLE 1

COMPARISON OF DEMOCRATIC PRIMARY ELECTORATE AND DEMOCRATIC GENERAL ELECTORATE, 1976, Percentages of Voters

	Less Than High School Education		*Black*		*Over Age 65*		*College Degree or Beyond*		*Income over $20,000/yr.*	
State	Primary	General	Primary	General	Primary	General	Primary	General	Primary	General
California	11	27	12	15	9	19	34	17	35	23
Florida	13	30	8	14	23	28	28	17	26	16
Illinois	19	34	15	16	8	17	23	6	25	21
Indiana	21	40	10	11	7	24	13	6	17	11
Massachusetts	12	19	2	3	10	18	36	22	24	24
Michigan	20	30	11	22	11	17	20	10	16	17
New Hampshire	11	18	—	—	6	13	38	18	15	14
New Jersey	12	41	17	26	9	16	35	14	37	19
New York	15	31	15	20	15	14	32	19	32	16
Ohio	15	32	11	17	7	19	25	10	23	17
Oregon	19	18	n.a.	n.a.	23	13	23	20	15	23
Pennsylvania	17	32	8	15	9	15	23	15	20	9
Wisconsin	18	25	3	7	13	19	22	15	n.a.	n.a.

NOTE: n.a. signifies data are not available.

SOURCE: Democratic Party, Commission on Presidential Nomination and Party Structure, "Openness, Participation and Party Building: Reforms for a Stronger Democratic Party," Washington, D.C., January 25, 1978, pp. 11-13.

called the Winograd Commission).[31] As Key says, "If 90 percent of the potential electorate shares in the nomination of candidates, obviously a different sort of political order exists than if only 10 percent of the maximum possible number of participants . . . [goes] to the polls on primary day." [32] The actual figures for recent years fall in between: in 1976, by Austin Ranney's reckoning, about half of those eligible turned out in primaries as turned out in the general election (28 percent versus 53.3 percent in competitive primary states).[33]

The literature on this subject has grown rich and complex, and for my purposes it would constitute a digression to explore it further. I only wish to establish a prima facie case for the proposition that the mass persuasion system that has effectively replaced party elites as the mechanism for selecting presidential nominees, especially in the Democratic party, comes with a significant price tag attached, and that its preferability cannot be established unequivocally by the straightforward invocation of the desideratum of participation. The gains and costs of this new system should, consequently, be carefully explored and considered by observers.

Political Consequences of Mass Decision Making

In this final section I shall discuss some general properties of decision making in a political system in which mass persuasion replaces elite persuasion. The discussion will probably strike some readers as extreme, even alarmist. I hasten to say, therefore, that I am trying to generate some ideas by exploring the consequences of an ideal type, related to, but abstracted from, rather more complicated realities. Let us imagine ourselves into a world that looks a great deal like the United States, but where more-or-less representative elites have a lot less to do, and referenda, plebiscites, direct voting mechanisms, and other manifestations of public opinion carry a greater burden of consequential decision making. What follows?

1. *Crazes or manias.* The intensity of short-term trends of opinion are amplified. Political leaders may come to believe that certain behavior is strongly demanded of them when it in fact has only weak or transitory support in the populace. In the 1950s, it was

[31] "Openness, Participation and Party Building: Reforms for a Stronger Democratic Party," Washington, D.C., January 25, 1978, pp. 11-13.

[32] *State Politics*, p. 134.

[33] *Participation in American Presidential Nominations, 1976* (Washington, D.C.: American Enterprise Institute, 1977), p. 25.

believed that the American population supported Senator Joseph McCarthy to a much greater degree than they actually did. Elites tended to interpret the movement of small straws as evidence of a big wind.

2. *Fads or social contagion.* This implies the geographic spread of sentiments (both real and imputed) from areas where they exist to areas where they do not. I am tempted to interpret the "Proposition 13" epidemic in this light. Real estate prices have not skyrocketed everywhere in the presence of multi-billion-dollar state government surpluses. There is, however, no Mann Act for ideas, forbidding the interstate transportation of immature notions for immoral purposes. Rather, there is the tendency for issue entrepreneurs to try their luck in one constituency after another, rather like burglars rattling all the doorknobs in a neighborhood, looking for weak defenses. Low turnouts in a referendum can constitute just such a weakness.

3. *The resuscitation of ideology.* I interpret the term *ideology* broadly to mean doctrines that elites invoke to capture the attention and compliance of masses. Presumably, elite politics in a mass-persuasion system consists of fights for control over the attention of publics. This includes conflict over the right to interpret equivocal or incoherent events—as most are—authoritatively. For example, an incident of urban violence is generally an incoherent event. Does it "mean" that there is too much racism in society, or that there are not enough police in the slums? Are looters expressing legitimate social grievances, or should they be shot?

4. *Reduced accountability.* The above point suggests that elites do not disappear under a mass persuasion system. They are, however, less accountable to one another and more subject to the constraints of popular fashion. They must learn to feed the mass media successfully, to cultivate different virtues, such as less patience, à la Richard Daley, and more indignation, à la Ralph Nader. Interest groups that organize themselves around such anachronisms as state and local party systems are bound to lose out to those that are skilled in currying favor with reporters and news media gatekeepers.

5. *Heroes and bums.* Such a system runs on name recognition, on celebrity, and on typecasting. Perhaps the most startling similarity between elite persuasion and mass persuasion systems is the inside track *both* give to children of the prominent who want to pursue political careers, but they give it through different mechanisms. In a mass system, name recognition is of great significance in the competition to overcome the inattentiveness of mass participants. Politicians must put enormous effort into structuring the ways in which they

are presented by and to the news media, since getting caught on the wrong side of something typecasts a political figure and makes him fair game. Henry Jackson and Morris Udall, two nearly identical liberal Democrats according to their records of thirty years' service and more in the Congress, were, respectively, the far right and far left Democratic presidential hopefuls of 1976. This, I suggest, was a dramaturgical necessity of mass persuasion politics; it had very little to do with their approach to most political issues.

The interesting problem of social control that I believe emerges from these reflections has to do with establishing accountability to the enduring values of a democratic society in elites that gain power in systems of mass persuasion. In the system of multiple elites evolved under the United States Constitution, accountability was maintained mostly by means of the checks and balances explicitly built into the machinery of government, and by means of a party system that structured the alternatives for electoral choice. It seems to me desirable to think again about the issue of checks and balances in the light of newly emerging centers of power that are taking the place of parties in the nomination process.

5
On the Three Parties in America

Robert A. Licht

Of all the species of human strife, politics most nearly resembles peace. In whatever system men have devised to govern themselves, or to rule others, it has been necessary first to understand and then to devise ways to contain or ameliorate the underlying profound conflicts of political life. These conflicts are perhaps exemplified by what has been called the "various and unequal distribution of property" or the conflict of rich and poor, of "the few" and "the many." Where there is a failure to understand the elements of strife and to devise the proper solutions, political institutions cannot be well-founded; no matter how lofty its goals—liberty, equality, justice, virtue, piety—the regime will not endure.

James Madison, in the justly celebrated *Federalist*, No. 10, reveals the understanding of the problems of strife, which he calls "faction," on the basis of which the American, or Madisonian, system of political liberty was founded:

> There are two methods of curing the mischiefs of faction: the one, by removing its causes; the other, by controlling its effects. There are again two methods of removing the causes of faction: the one, by destroying the liberty which is essential to its existence; the other, by giving to every citizen the same opinions, the same passions, and the same interests.[1]

As to removing the causes, Madison held that "the second expedient is as impracticable as the first would be unwise." The preferred solution, rather, is to control the effects of faction.

---

[1] *The Federalist* (New York: Modern Library, 1964), p. 54.

The late Martin Diamond, one of the most incisive students of the American founding, instructs us wisely about Madison's thought:

> Madison's search for the solution to the democratic problem . . . led him to envisage and help found the extended, commercial, democratic republic. Always before the politics of democracy had flowed naturally into the fatal factionalism deriving from opinion, passion, and class interest. . . . Employing the "new science of politics," Madison discovered in "interest" its latent possibility, that is, a novel way of channeling the stream of politics away from these natural directions and toward that kind of factionalism with which a democracy could cope, namely a politics of "various and interfering interests."[2]

The American political system, based upon the "new science of politics," is laid down in the Constitution. The Constitution embodies the politics of "various and interfering interests" and is the basis for curing the "mischiefs of faction." The federal system with its vast extension of sovereignty and strong national government, the principle of representation (which Madison identifies with the word "republic"),[3] the separation of powers, the Bill of Rights—all are the safeguards of the goals of the regime: liberty, equality, and justice.

The above list, however, is incomplete without the inclusion of the political parties. Although extraconstitutional, it may be said that the parties emerged naturally and inevitably to serve and become part of the political system. As Jeane Kirkpatrick has observed, "democratic parties remain instruments of private persons shaping and controlling government rather than agencies of the government whose function is to shape the society."[4] Through the parties, the political virtues vital to the republic—compromise, accommodation, and moderation—become active and widespread.

The American political parties are each broad-based coalitions of many and diverse interests, necessarily sharing many features even while they are divided on important issues of public policy. They are not based upon narrow ideologies, nor are they divided by grand and opposing principles.

---

[2] Martin Diamond, "Ethics and Politics: The American Way," in Robert H. Horwitz, ed., *The Moral Foundations of the American Republic* (Charlottesville: University of Virginia Press, 1977), pp. 39-72. See also Robert A. Licht, "Reflections on Martin Diamond's *Ethics and Politics*, etc." *Publius*, vol. 8, no. 3 (Summer 1978).

[3] *The Federalist*, p. 59.

[4] Jeane J. Kirkpatrick, *Dismantling the Parties: Reflections on Party Reform and Party Decomposition* (Washington, D.C.: American Enterprise Institute, 1979), p. 22.

The history of party politics in America has been mostly benign.[5] The battle over the privilege of governing has not been to the death. Defeat has not been final, nor victory enduring. The American democracy appears to have acquired, through the vital agency of the parties, the aristocratic capacity to govern and be governed in turn.

Now, however, as the essays in this volume and elsewhere make abundantly clear, the parties appear to have entered a period of disintegration with few prospects of vital reorganization. Some say the decline is terminal. Many wonder what the larger consequences must be for our institutions. Others in this volume see the present state of affairs as either good in itself because the parties are themselves barriers to the true idea of American democracy, or good because it derives from reforms that are fundamentally healthy.

The present essay inclines toward the pessimistic view that the present state of the political parties portends an unraveling of what shall here be called the polity. However, this essay also differs markedly from others in this volume in its approach to the problem of the political parties.

The "three parties in America" does not mean the Democratic, Republican, and some unnamed third party. Rather, "parties" here means something different and more fundamental, namely, *parts* of a whole or, perhaps more precisely still, the *elements* of faction. For the present political parties, although in a sense essential for the health of the republic, cannot be said to be its elements or parts from which the whole is constituted. They are at best contingent, as their present turmoil makes clear. Moreover, they have been so successful precisely because they obscure the underlying conflicts; the parties have been part of the solution to the problem of faction because they are part of the politics of "various and interfering interests."

The three parties or elements are *democracy, oligarchy,* and *aristocracy*. The use to which these terms will be put is novel in the present context, but not new in the history of political thought. They derive from the "old" political science which was supplanted by the new. If the "new" political science of the Founders effected a "cure" to the "mischiefs of faction," the old science may yet serve to reveal the disease for which the new science is a cure. In the course of this essay, it is hoped that the meaning of this new but old vocabulary will become clear.

[5] Henry Jones Ford observed that the political parties were "the last bond of union to give way" in the face of the "crisis of the house divided"—the Civil War. Quoted in Edward C. Banfield, "In Defense of the American Party System," in Robert A. Goldwin, ed., *Political Parties, U.S.A.* (Chicago: Rand McNally, 1961), pp. 21-39.

Democracy and Oligarchy

As we all know, America is a middle-class nation. No very great sociological sophistication is required to recognize the truthful quality of this assertion. At first, however, it might appear that to have said as much is really to have said very little. Nevertheless, what will be argued here is that the middle-class character of the United States, when properly understood, is a political fact of the greatest moment. Indeed, it would scarcely be an exaggeration to say that a numerous and thriving middle class is *the* American solution to the problem of an enduring polity.

But we are so accustomed to the term "middle class," its part in our lives is so pervasive and its extent so vast, that perhaps its true significance for understanding American politics may no longer be visible to us. It is necessary, therefore, to try to step back and gain some perspective. For this purpose it will be instructive to examine briefly the writings of men who, in different degrees, were strangers to our ways.

Alexis de Tocqueville, a Frenchman of aristocratic birth whose very considerable intellectual gifts were bent to the task of understanding the new democratic order that had forever changed his world, understood very well the special qualities—we should call them "middling" qualities—that are distinctively American:

> The first thing that strikes a traveler in the United States is the innumerable multitude of those who seek to emerge from their original condition; and the second is the rarity of lofty ambition to be observed in the midst of the universally ambitious stir of society. No Americans are devoid of a yearning desire to rise, but hardly any appear to entertain hopes of a great magnitude or to pursue very lofty aims. All are constantly seeking to acquire property, power and reputation; few contemplate these things upon a great scale.[6]

One may find in *Democracy in America* many similarly revealing passages in which Tocqueville seeks to show the special "middling" character of men formed in the American mold. That this mold reflected Madison's politics of "various and interfering interests" is visible, for example, in Tocqueville's famous chapter on "How the Americans Combat Individualism by the Principle of Self-Interest Rightly Understood."

---

[6] Alexis de Tocqueville, *Democracy in America*, ed. Phillips Bradley (New York: Alfred A. Knopf, 1956), vol. 2, ch. 19, p. 243.

Tocqueville located the cause of the special American qualities in the egalitarian, or what he called democratic, temper of the United States. But his observations about the relation of the middle class and equality, although based upon his novel experiences of the new world, were hardly original. Indeed, the importance of the middle class was quite well known to the old science of politics.

Although Aristotle never knew anything like America, he showed in his *Politics* that equality and the middle class were related in an important way:

> A *polis* [that is, a "city" or self-contained political entity] aims at being, as far as it can be, composed of men equal and alike; and the middle class, more than any other, has this sort of composition.[7]

Although the middle class may be composed of men "equal and alike," Aristotle does not draw the conclusion that it is simply "democratic." His way of analysis is quite different from our accustomed thought. In Aristotle's view, the middle class lies between the democratic element and another, which he calls the "oligarchic," because it is neither very poor nor very rich:

> In all states [*poleis*] there may be distinguished three parts, or classes . . . the very rich; the very poor; and the middle class which forms the mean. Now it is admitted as a general principle, that moderation and the mean are always best. We may therefore conclude that in the ownership of all the gifts of fortune a middle condition will be the best. Men who are in this condition are the most ready to listen to reason.

For Aristotle, the middling condition of middle-class men is a prognosis of good health for the polity:

> Those who belong to either extreme—the exceedingly beautiful, exceedingly strong, exceedingly well-born or exceedingly rich, or the opposite of these, the exceedingly beggarly, exceedingly weak or very ignoble—find it hard to follow the lead of reason.

Men of the extremes, they tend to extremes. Bold, insolent, dangerously ambitious, and ruined by luxury, on the one side, and, on the other, given to petty criminality and servility and made mean

---

[7] This discussion is found in Aristotle, *The Politics*, trans. Ernest Barker (New York: Oxford University Press, 1962), bk. 4, ch. 11, passim. I am indebted to Prof. Laurence Berns's forthcoming translation of *The Politics* for a few alterations in Barker's translation. I alone, of course, am responsible for these changes.

spirited by poverty, the men of the extremes neither govern themselves nor are fit to govern others or be governed. One extreme is contemptuous while the other is envious.

A middle class, because of its moderate prosperity, Aristotle speaks of as both secure—not coveting the property of others—and politically stable: "Neither plotting against others, nor plotted against themselves, they live in freedom from danger." Lest we believe this last to be simply a statement of existing conditions, it is followed immediately by the prayer of Phocylides: "Many things are best for the middling; gladly would I be of the polis' middle class."

So Aristotle would not call a political system in which the middle class is numerous and active a "democracy" simply, for that in his view is the name of an extreme. Rather, he calls it a "polity," or "mixture" of democracy and oligarchy. His esteem for this kind of polity must surprise us if we remember only his teaching about the very best, aristocratic republic of "virtue."[8] A middle-class polity he calls the best for the majority of men and states. It is hard, in Aristotle's scheme, to give a name other than "polity" to a middle-class regime; ambiguity is a mark of excellence:

> It is a good criterion of a proper mixture of democracy and oligarchy that a polity should be able to be described indifferently as either. When this can be said, it must obviously be due to the excellence of the mixture.

Aristotle extends to this polity praise of which Madison would have approved: "[The middle class polity] is the one type free from faction; where the middle class is large, there is least likelihood of faction and dissension among its citizens."[9]

Now that we have reminded ourselves of Madison, however, it is also necessary to indicate how very far we, the political descendants

[8] See also Paul Eidelberg, *The Philosophy of the American Constitution: A Reinterpretation of the Intentions of the Founders* (New York: The Free Press, 1968). This interesting book was brought to my attention just when this article was nearly completed. The author argues that the intention of the Founders was to establish a "mixed regime" of the classical type—i.e., one with democratic, oligarchic, aristocratic, and monarchical elements whose goal, if not simply "virtue," cannot be completed without it. Full justice to the author's elaborate and learned argument cannot be done here. However, my own view at present is more modest. To be sure, the regime is a "polity," that is, is "mixed," but that mixture is primarily of the oligarchic and democratic elements. It remains an open question whether this polity was fully *intended* by the Founders, or whether they may be said to have solved what I, following Aristotle, believe to be a "natural" problem of political self-rule. Moreover, as regards "virtue," the reader will see that in my view, the polity fails to solve its "aristocratic" problem.

[9] Aristotle, *Politics*, bk. 4, ch. 11.

of Madison, are from Aristotle, for the middle-class polity, in Aristotle's experience, was an exceedingly rare species. Indeed, to him it seemed destined to fail more often than to succeed, even in those very few places where it managed to begin a precarious existence. The reason for this seems to lie in the fact that the middle class was small and relatively weak. In the ongoing struggle of the democracy and the oligarchy, of the poor against the rich, whichever gained the ascendancy altered the constitution to its advantage. Perhaps the struggle between the elements was simply intractable when left to is own inertial movements: ". . . no matter which side may win the day, it refuses to establish a polity based upon the common interest and the principle of equality." This explained to Aristotle, in part, "why a middle or mixed type of constitution has never been established—or, at the most, has only been established on a few occasions and in a few states."

We, who in our many millions, live, move, and have our being in the life of the middle class and can only with difficulty imagine any other life must be struck with wonder at the changes that created our world.

From our perspective a solution to Aristotle's problem of how to create a polity of the middle class might appear to be simply stated. Since the problem is the weakness of the middle class relative to the poor and the rich, the middle class must be strengthened, that is, its numbers must be increased and the extremes of poverty and wealth reduced. One thing above all seems necessary for increasing the numbers of the middle class. That is to increase the wealth of the community, thereby, it is hoped, creating access to wealth for the poor. If, however, the poor were to enter the middle class simply by confiscating the wealth of the rich, a conflict must once again arise between the extremes, and the total wealth also would not increase. Similarly, if the rich alone were to benefit from the increase in wealth, the same conflict must result, and the outlook for wealth, where it does not solve but only exacerbates the political problem, is dim.

Although we may state the solution with simplicity—the middle class must be strengthened, for which an increase in the wealth of the community is a prerequisite—this requires steps which were beyond the limits vital to Aristotle's larger thought.

Today we are at ease with the thought of increasing the wealth of nations. Such a thought, however, posits an end to natural scarcity, the basis of human poverty. This requires, in turn, that the pursuit and creation of wealth be established as one of the most desirable of political goals. An end to natural scarcity by human agency, and the creation of wealth as a goal of polity, are in fact radical alterations for Aristotelian thought.

The creation of wealth effectively means an increase in the exploitation of nature and in human productivity. We call these increases by the general name of technology. Our technology, however, is based upon a science of nature fundamentally different from Aristotle's. Indeed, rather than technology's being based upon science, our science may well have come into existence for the sake of exploiting nature and increasing human productivity, however autonomous the glories of its theoretical system may appear.

The change of goals of polity to accommodate the necessity of producing wealth is also a fundamental change in moral outlook. This change is synonymous with a new understanding of man. Without this new understanding the American Founding cannot itself be understood.

Aristotle's thought, however, rests upon a twofold understanding of nature and the nature of man, which forms a virtually insurmountable barrier to the establishment of a polity of the middle class as we know and live it, although not necessarily to every form of middle-class polity.

This brief and necessarily incomplete look at the middle-class polity may serve a useful purpose in a discussion of the American political parties or, in more general but more precise terms, the problem of faction. For example, we may now see that the middle class may be viewed as a solution to the problem of faction and, further, that in it are revealed the true elements of faction, or the "parts" from which the political whole is constituted.

In essence, the middle class, then, may be seen as a political creation; not, perhaps, so much in terms of its origins, which may well be accidental, but of its function. As a political creation, the middle class can be eliminated, which has been the aim of virtually all radical democratic regimes of our time and of the ideologies upon which they rest. It may also be enlarged, which has been the goal of all liberal polities. To defend the middle class has become literally a matter of life and death for the liberal polities. But it is obvious that, although perhaps the preeminent feature of the landscape of the liberal polities of our time, the middle class has not fared well in terms of political thought. To this matter we must return later. At this juncture, however, it is necessary to turn to the problem of faction in the United States.

As we noted earlier, the pervasiveness of the middle class in the United States obscures the elements of faction. Nevertheless, it is possible to detect the factions in shadows cast by the institutions designed to cure the "mischiefs of faction." It is possible, for example, to speak of the Republican and Democratic parties as tending, respectively, in the directions of "oligarchy" and "democracy." At the same time, it is clearly not possible to name them as such unequivocally. They are each a "mixture," or, as we observed earlier, parts of the middle-class solution, rather than the elements of faction.

The elements continue to live on as well in the rhetoric of party reform, which fact may engage the interests of those who study ironies. The call for reform, when reduced to its essence, pits "the people" against "the interests." Indeed, this rhetoric is part of a kind of populist revival at the present time. Like so much of American political rhetoric, however, there is a sense in which it is out of phase with the observed phenomena. The most obvious objection to it is that it is difficult to distinguish the people from the interests. Even so, it would be short-sighted to ignore rhetoric of such proven destructive power.

The struggle of the people against the interests, even if only a quarrel in speech, is the lineal descendant of the quarrel between the oligarchs and democrats. "The people," in antiquity, were called "the many." The rule of the many is what the term "democracy" means. In the nature of things, the many were generally, in some degree, also the poor. "The interests," on the other hand, clearly refers to those who possess property to the degree that the protection of it becomes a matter of political organization. Anciently it was the rule of "the few," or "oligarchy," when this faction had political power.

As Aristotle explained in his *Politics*, however, the key to understanding the dispute was not to be found in the numbers:

> We have defined democracy as the sovereignty of numbers; but we can conceive of a case in which the majority who hold the sovereignty . . . are the well-to-do. Similarly oligarchy is generally stated to be the sovereignty of a small number; but it might conceivably happen that the poorer classes were fewer in number than the well-to-do, and yet—in virtue of superior vigour—were the sovereign authority . . . The real ground of the difference between oligarchy and democracy is poverty and riches.[10]

---

[10] Ibid., bk. 3, ch. 8.

But it is of the essence of a political quarrel that justice is alleged to be on each side. Aristotle merely said the obvious when he observed that, as regards the oligarchs and democrats, each party's idea of justice was a consequence of its political interests and therefore defective. For each judged its own case, "and most men, as a rule, are bad judges where their own interests are involved." But there is another and deeper reason why the respective ideas of justice were defective:

> They [democrats and oligarchs] are misled by the fact that they are professing a sort of conception of justice, and professing it up to a point, into thinking that they profess one which is absolute and complete. The oligarchs think that superiority on one point—in their case wealth—means superiority on all: the democrats believe that equality in one respect—for instance, that of free birth—means equality all around.

And this quarrel over equality and inequality inevitably leads to the question of merit:

> Justice is relative to persons; and a just distribution is one in which the relative values of the things given correspond to those of the person receiving . . . But the advocates of oligarchy and democracy, while they agree about what constitutes equality in the *thing*, disagree about what constitutes it in *persons*.[11]

Nothing in this description of the quarrel over equality and merit is unfamiliar to us. What is surprising, in fact, when we look at ourselves candidly, is the extent to which both sides of the quarrel are enmeshed in our political life.

To this point, however, a crucial qualification must be added. For us the question of "right" is held to be at the center of the questions of equality and merit. At the present time, one of the most important political quarrels in our land is over the degree to which both equalities and inequalities are legitimated by the idea of rights.

The distinction, then, between the people and the interests is not mere rhetoric, latent as it is with the most enduring of political quarrels and challenges to the polity. It is, however, a distinction obscured among us by the fact that everyone believes himself a "democrat," if only for the reason that no one will accept the label of "oligarch" as being truly descriptive of his political opinions. Everyone, whether he wishes to protect his property or to see that

---

[11] Ibid., bk. 3, ch. 9.

of others redistributed, believes himself to act in behalf of "democracy." Our quarrels are not bloody for the reason that both parties aspire to the "middle class" and because, for us, "democrat" does not mean "propertyless." Both the people and the interests are one in having interests, possessing property or wishing to acquire it and all the goods of liberal, that is, middle-class, life. And both believe they have a "right" to the things for which they hope. Both share, therefore, a common if ambivalent language, and this, at least, reflects Aristotle's dictum that "a properly mixed polity should look as if it contained both democratic and oligarchical elements—and as if it contained neither."

The American democracy then may perhaps best be described as an *oligarchical democracy,* although to say this requires more candor than prudently we should have. The quarrel between these elements, or factions, is for us only potential, although, through a variety of causes, it could well become actual. The American democracy is a successful mixture of two of its constituent elements. A sign of the success of the mixture is the fact that the elements only become visible upon the destruction of the polity. The political parties, to repeat, are the evidence that this quarrel has not degenerated into the disease of faction.

The creation of this polity is based upon the idea of interests that are primarily economic. In this fact is found the politics of enlightened self-interest, whose roots run deep in the political philosophy of the Founders. They saw in an extended commercial republic, with its potentially vast diversity of economic interests, a substitute for the irreconcilable nature of religious and morally based political divisions, as Martin Diamond has so eloquently shown. The foundation of political unity and stability, therefore, was laid, paradoxically, in a multiplicity of interests. Economic interests are, in principle, reconcilable because they are governed by an operative justice that commands virtually universal assent. The case for moral and religious conflict is far less certain.

The guarantee of religious liberty and the disestablishment of religion together were the means chosen by the Founders to defuse and "depoliticize" religious conflict, or conflict based upon moral conviction. This encouraged a multiplicity of sects, as it was intended to do, while giving to none official sanction with its consequent domination of moral opinion.

This solution has brought about what might be called a soft consensus on religious and moral matters, which is best called by the name of liberal religion. It has also generated a widespread disdain for the rule of religion in the formation of character and, therefore, in everyday matters.

Into this partial vacuum has grown what might be called alternative moralities. The most prominent "moral" issues of recent decades —race and minorities, including homosexuals; abortion; equal rights for women; and ecology and the environment—have confused and altered the soft consensus. Whether, therefore, the safe and moderate solution of the Founders can endure remains an open question.

Nevertheless, in the confusion of moral claims on political life, it is possible to speak of a common public morality that suffuses our political discourse. This public morality, of course, is egalitarianism, and it is rooted in the governing idea of our political system, in the idea of rights.

American egalitarianism, however, is not one thing but two. In this it reflects the polity of oligarchic democracy. There is equality simply, or, as it is variously called, equality of condition or of outcomes. This may be called the purely democratic understanding of equality. Defenders of this view often argue that inequality is the consequence only of unfair, that is, unjust, advantage and bad fortune, and that it is within the power of the laws to correct and to restore the "natural" condition.

On the other hand, there is the oligarchic version of equality, which we call equality of opportunity. It sanctions inequalities of wealth, position, and influence. Its defenders argue that "right" follows from unequal effort, ability, and frugality. They tend to overlook the central fact of good fortune in all prosperity and its inequalities and to overestimate the part that ability plays.

The public morality favors the oligarchic version. It shapes our lives and is essentially moderate. It legitimates a range of inequalities in our national life, including the very idea of representative government based upon election rather than by casting lots.

The two versions of egalitarianism are not necessarily incompatible. If "equality simply" is defined as equality before the law and if the law sanctions certain inequalities, it is compatible with equality of opportunity. But if equality of condition means equality in all things, or "radical" equality, and if the law is interpreted or rewritten to assure this outcome, then it is not compatible with equality of opportunity. The twofold sense of equality therefore reflects ambiguities that exacerbate tensions inherent in the polity, as can be seen in the quarrel over affirmative action.[12]

---

[12] The proponents of affirmative action are ambivalent about its meaning. We do not know if, in their ambivalence, there is to be found a qualified acquiescence

Democracy may thus be said to be the fulcrum on which the American polity turns, but its lever is oligarchy. This oligarchy, however, is profoundly qualified by democracy. Equality of opportunity is, after all, still equality primarily. The polity is "middle class," and the kind of equality it fosters reflects this. The allure of the oligarchic democracy, or the polity of the middle class, is that it seeks to satisfy the natural desires for inequality as well as equality and that such a polity cuts across all racial and ethnic differences.[13]

---

in the idea of oligarchic democracy and thus a source of conciliation with their opponents. They desire equality of outcome insofar as there should be proportional representation in the professions and skilled trades. But they also desire equality of starting position, or condition, by means of numerical quotas, as if unequal contestants were being handicapped in a race. But is the race for career, success, and advantage, that is, oligarchic advantage? Were there no such advantage to be derived, that is, no inequalities, would there be a motive for affirmative action?

Affirmative action might therefore seem to advance the cause of oligarchic democracy. But it is deeply flawed as regards justice. The flaw lies in the fact that a principle of equity—the division of material goods, of "things"—is conflated with the principle of distributive justice—of "persons"—which requires that unequal things be given to unequals. The rancor of the dispute is thereby generated by the inherent tension over "merit." The distributive principle may be called an aristocratic idea of justice because it rewards "the best," or excellence. Its place in the conflict, however, is undermined because the oligarchic position on merit is compromised. The true issue, after all, is not rewarding the best, or excellence for its own sake, but advantage, or opportunity.

[13] The foregoing account might be thought to overlook the problem of "race" in our political conflicts, a problem potentially indigestible by the polity. This, it is sometimes thought, is the true meaning of affirmative action. Perhaps this is so, but the allure of the oligarchic democracy, or the polity of the middle class that seeks to satisfy the natural desires for both equality and inequality, cuts across all racial differences. Race is indeed a serious problem for the polity, but not for the reasons usually given.

The racial struggle in the United States may be divided into roughly three phases: abolition, which established the universality of the principle of equality; civil rights, which sought to eliminate all residual legal disabilities that were impediments to full equality; and the transformation of civil rights into the battle for racial justice. The first two were fought over the correct interpretation and implementation of our principles, and to eliminate the issue of race, thereby permitting the polity to expand and embrace all. The last, however, claimed that "racism" is endemic in the United States, which is a "racist" society. The barriers to full civil rights, therefore, in principle were insurmountable without the complete reform of society. The practical effects of this claim are surely pernicious. They include the central element of affirmative action, namely, the theory of coercive compensation for past wrongs based solely upon race or minority status.

"Racial justice" is not a theory that wells up, unbidden by thought, out of the mere "fact" of race. Like any other theory, its basis is thought, and it is the work of mind. It is, therefore, the work of a class of people whose life is defined by thought, and such men and women are not confined to any particular skin color. To the extent that this class articulates a systematic and irreconcilable opposition to the political order, they must be considered a true element of political strife. It is the assimilation of *this* element into the polity that is the issue, not race.

This is not to deny that there is a residual democratic class in America that is defined by its relative poverty and marginal access to wealth and office. The innately prudential response of American politics has been, using the lever of oligarchy, to seek to enfranchise this class and to raise it to the "middle." There is also a class that may well be "oligarchic," possessing wealth and influence somewhat disproportionate to that of the rest of the polity. It, too, is residual. In this fact, namely that the extremes are reduced in numbers and significance without having to be enslaved or "liquidated," may be found the health of the polity.

Oligarchy and Aristocracy

The search for the "elements" may not stop at oligarchy and democracy. There is a third party—aristocracy—of signal importance in any discussion of the American polity and its potential factions.

As wealth accumulates and is inherited, leisure and the possibility of cultivation emerge, and an aristocracy arises. In the past, the aristocracy bred the "gentleman," the man of cultivated leisure. In the American oligarchic democracy this natural process, although clearly present, is arrested. Virtually no one will accept the label "aristocrat," and although the term "gentleman" once had some standing, it has gradually become obsolete. These terms have just about no public legitimacy; journalists do use the term "patrician"—from the old Roman senatorial aristocracy—to distinguish certain persons from the merely wealthy, but without political signification.

The best of the patrician families have been formed and inspired by the idea of public service and by the American and liberal idea of philanthropy. They wish to see the ordinary man progress while they try to limit the access of the parvenu to their families and society. Excluding the oligarchy, however, is difficult. There are no titles or other such symbols of unyielding exclusivity, and it often takes very little time for oligarchic ambition and achievement to culminate in inherited wealth. Virtually all American fortunes may be traced back to some entrepreneurial activity of the not very remote past. If wealth, whose basis is commerce and not land, is to be preserved, the ties between the old money and the new must be kept green and growing. Only shrewd and entrepreneurial management can avoid the ultimate dispersal of fortunes through inheritance taxes, incompetence, and profligacy. If a "gentleman" wishes to avoid impoverishment, the fortune must be managed in the American manner, that is, the heirs must acquire entrepreneurial ambition, which is an impediment to leisure and cultivation.

But the most telling barrier to the emergence of a self-consciously aristocratic class is the fact that uncultivated idleness is debilitating in a land of oligarchic ambition. America is governed by ambition, and offers few inducements to aristocratic cultivation.

Cultivation is of the essence of aristocracy, which is defined by the qualities it cultivates. Traditionally, these have been defined as moral and intellectual excellence, or "virtue," guided by some dominant opinion about what constitutes "the best" in man. The function of an aristocracy in the polity, therefore, was to conserve these received and dominant opinions by making them live in every generation. This was the basis of the aristocratic share of rule within the polity.

The aristocracy, therefore, has traditionally been the class that cultivated the natural talent necessary for providing a future generation of leaders. The numerous enemies of this class quite understandably saw this as merely the protection of privilege. In England, for example, the aristocracy drew the pool of talent from within its own ranks for very many generations. The Catholic church, on the other hand, is said to have functioned as an instrument for cultivating the talent to be found throughout the classes. Such talent constitutes what Thomas Jefferson called a "natural aristocracy." He distinguished it sharply from what he called the "pseudo-aristocracy" or what, with less contempt, might be called a traditional or conventional aristocracy. In this distinction Jefferson merely followed the lead of Aristotle, who observed that common usage tended mistakenly to identify oligarchy with aristocracy.[14]

The term "natural aristocracy," because of the democratic temper of the United States, enjoys no currency. Nevertheless, we are to a degree obsessed with the idea of "gifted individuals." We find ways and means, as do most nations, to cultivate and expand this pool of the most intelligent, the most talented, the best, the *aristoi*. Egalitarianism, however, requires that we view this process within the horizon of equality of opportunity, and that no "class" interest be encouraged to emerge. Thus we use the sociological jargon term "elite" to describe rather indiscriminately this class. "Elite" appears to be a scientifically neutral term that has also been politically neutered, since it carries with it few of the traditional associations of aristocracy. Unfortunately, neither does it signify unequivocally "the best." Hitler's SS, for example, is said to have been an elite. So the term is neither scientifically precise nor politically neutral, but

---

[14] Aristotle, *Politics*, bk. 4, ch. 8, passim.

often functions as a term of abuse in the quasiscientific rhetoric of democracy.

The American Founders rejected implicitly a place in the polity for a cultivated aristocratic class, one set apart as a conventional or "pseudo" aristocracy. They rejected the opinion that the only sound basis for popular republican institutions is "virtue." This they supplanted with the notion of enlightened self-interest, a principle which, as Tocqueville observed, "produces no great acts of self-sacrifice, but . . . suggests daily small acts of self-denial." In fact, as he shows, rightly understood, self-interest is an answer to mere selfishness and unyielding individualism, habituating men to certain virtues, even if they are not lofty.

The separation of self-interest from moral opinion as the sound foundation of popular government also set free acquisitiveness from the strictures of received morality and came close to making it positively admirable. If this served to weaken the grip of the received moral opinions, all the more did it tend to disinherit and disfranchise the aristocracy, who were the conservators and embodiment of the dominant moral opinions and who, traditionally, have disdained the cultivation of acquisitiveness.

Although the conventional aristocracy was largely destroyed as a class, we must not overlook the extent to which the natural aristoi were set free from the rule of received opinion. Jefferson called this fund of talent "the most precious gift of nature for the instruction, the trusts, and government of society."[15] His famous scheme for education in Virginia was aimed at separating out the best whom, he said, would "be raked from the rubbish." Most importantly, he saw in this the key to the health of the polity: "That form of government is best," he wrote, "which provides the most effectually for a pure selection of these natural aristoi into the offices of government."[16]

There can be no question that the American Founders were just such gifted men, natural aristoi nurtured in the old conventions but freed from them by thought. It might be believed that they wrote themselves and their kind out of the Constitution because they devised a system that would not require the continued presence of men like themselves in order to remain free and self-governing. This, however, is somewhat misleading. Not only did the Founders succeed in changing the meaning of popular government by setting it upon new foun-

[15] Thomas Jefferson, *Notes on The State of Virginia* (New York: Harper and Row, 1964), p. 140.

[16] *The Adams-Jefferson Letters*, ed. Lester J. Cappon (New York: Simon & Schuster, 1971), vol. 2, pp. 387-92.

dations, they achieved as well the enfranchisement of the natural aristocracy.

This enfranchisement was accomplished not by education, but by creating places within the polity for the aristoi to emerge without, at the same time, allowing a separate class interest to develop. The natural aristoi, instead, were to be cultivated by the peculiar machinery and demands of the oligarchic democracy. Two routes to this goal were provided: the first was government, and the second was the alliance of science with commerce and the numerous offspring of this union.

There are primarily two aristocratic elements within the separation of powers, the Senate and the judiciary. We, of course, do not ordinarily think of the Senate as an "aristocratic" chamber. The very name, however, conjures its aristocratic Roman antecedent, and the authors of *The Federalist* had thus to anticipate the objection that the Senate might be transformed "into a tyrannical aristocracy." Although the requirements for holding the office of senator are minimal—age and citizenship—*The Federalist* defends them on the ground of the nature of the "senatorial trust," which requires a "greater extent of information and stability of character." To speak of "information" and "character" is but another way of speaking of the old aristocratic intellectual and moral requirements that are indispensable to the Senate's stabilizing, or conserving, function. The Senate provides a reservoir of the knowledge of "the objects and principles of legislation":

> A good government implies two things; first *fidelity* to the object of government, which is the happiness of the people; secondly, a *knowledge* of the means by which that object can best be attained. (Emphasis added.)[17]

Knowledge must include foresight as to the far-reaching effects of legislation. Legislation may be proposed on the basis of a popular outcry and enthusiasm. Its remote consequences may well be harmful, however, and the foresight of the Senate acts as a check on this possibility. The chamber thus must be deliberative in the widest sense, for the rule of law is also the rule of reason.

The stability of the Senate, according to *The Federalist,* or its "fidelity" to the objects of government, provides the basis for "national character" which must govern the conduct of foreign affairs. "Every nation . . . whose affairs betray a want of wisdom and sta-

[17] *The Federalist,* p. 404. See especially Nos. 62 and 63.

bility" will be undone by "the more systematic policy of their wiser neighbors."

In the absence of "wisdom and stability" in domestic affairs, there can only be an uncertain course of legislation. Men will speculate against the future of such an uncertain course of legislation. This will encourage and let loose an extreme of what we may call oligarchic ambition. But if the course of legislation is wise and constant, the enterprising and industrious spirit of the middle class will be encouraged. Thus the "virtues" of the Senate further the interests of the polity by checking one of its extreme possibilities, while encouraging the "middle."

At the other extreme, the Senate acts as a check upon democratic instability: "Such institutions may be sometimes necessary as a defence to the people against their own temporary errors and delusions."

Finally, the senators are representatives of the "residuary sovereignty" of the states. They thus represent interests that cannot be defined as merely selfish and individualistic. Rather, they are interests rooted in the prudential preservation of sovereignty. The "stable and select body" that is the Senate provides the central place in the national government where the aristocratic capacity called prudence, or political wisdom, may be exercised and cultivated.

A somewhat different but no less aristocratic cultivation is afforded by the judiciary:

> There can be but few men in society who will have sufficient skill in the laws to qualify them for the station of judges. And making the proper deductions for the ordinary depravity of human nature, the number must be smaller still of those who unite the requisite integrity with the requisite knowledge.[18]

The courts also provide an essentially conserving function. In the Supreme Court the Constitution must be regarded as fundamental law. Jurisprudence looks backward to precedent and, ultimately, to this fundamental law. The capacity of jurisprudence differs from the prudence of the legislators, who must look forward to the remote consequences and are answerable for them, if only at the ballot box.

The point here is not whether the Senate and the judiciary are in fact observed to act in this aristocratic manner. We are all too familiar with the growing failure of deliberative reason in the Senate and with the fact that the highest court now legislates by abandoning

---

[18] Ibid., p. 510. See especially Nos. 78 and 79.

jurisprudence without acquiring political wisdom. Rather, the description of the Founders indicates the aristocratic function of these institutions within the governing mechanism of the polity, namely, the natural and necessary exercise of the moral and intellectual excellences requisite for self-government. The institutions provide the scope and opportunity for cultivating the required excellences; the polity requires them; and with fair frequency they are achieved.

The other route for the emergence of the natural aristoi is the alliance of science and commerce. As Lincoln said of the Patent Laws —which enshrine this alliance in the Constitution—they "added the fuel of *interest* to the *fire* of genius." [19] This alliance runs very deep in modern political thought and may be traced back to the idea of the "mastery of nature for the relief of man's estate" in the writings of Francis Bacon and others.[20]

For man to master nature, or to aim his best efforts—political, intellectual, and moral—at the relief of man's earthly estate, required that certain elements of his own nature be permitted to flourish which, in previous ages, were not thought to be the best in him. Modern liberalism, in joining together the ideas of self-interest and scientific benevolence, transformed the moral outlook. The moral idea of human progress justified and invigorated the intellectual endeavor. Modern science gave the intellectual abilities of the naturally talented a nearly limitless world of possibilities to explore and exploit, which, in turn, created vast new possibilities of material abundance for the mass of mankind fortunate enough to live where the ideas and practices of modern liberalism took root. The sheer numbers of the natural aristoi that could now emerge increased. Never has the quantity of intellectual work done in the world been so large as it is in our time. The idea of the scientist as the benefactor of mankind provided the moral impetus for this transformation.

It is commerce, however, that mediates between self-interest and scientific benevolence by turning the fruits of science to human benefit. Of course, this is now a cliché and is much resented by scientists, who do not regard themselves beholden to commerce. They might agree that prosperity is a requirement for liberty, but they do

[19] Abraham Lincoln, "On Discoveries and Inventions," Speech delivered Feb. 11, 1859, in *The Collected Works of Abraham Lincoln*, ed. Roy P. Basler (New Brunswick, N.J.: Rutgers University Press, 1953).

[20] A most valuable discussion of these matters is to be found in Richard Kennington's "Descartes and the Mastery of Nature," in S. F. Spicker, ed., *Organism, Medicine and Metaphysics* (Dordrecht, Holland: D. Reidel, 1978), pp. 201-23. Also see Laurence Berns, "Francis Bacon and The Conquest of Nature," *Interpretation*, vol. 7, no. 1 (Jan. 1978), and "Liberal and Illiberal Politics," *The Review of Politics*, vol. 40, no. 2 (April 1978).

not agree that commerce is a requirement for prosperity. The restiveness of the scientific aristocracy has become a most important political fact of our time.[21]

In any event, the moral merit of being a benefactor of mankind is inextricably linked to the intellectual merit of scientific inquiry, the protests of the "pure" scientists notwithstanding. The increase in prosperity based upon scientific inquiry is indispensable to a political liberty that is not based directly upon the older idea of virtue. Excellence of an intellectual kind is no longer the proper *goal* but the necessary *instrument* of political liberty. Similarly, the moral restraint of moderation, formerly sought for its own sake, gives way to the self-restraint of frugality and industriousness, the instrumental virtues.[22] This, at least, is how earlier, less hedonistic, and more optimistic times saw the matter.

The alliance of science and commerce naturally takes the form of large enterprises. As the place of science becomes more important the management of these enterprises is transformed from simply entrepreneurial to "scientific" management. The excellence of the "manager" of the corporation increasingly imitates that of the statesman. The corporation as a mode of commerce is a quasiautonomous entity. Having elements of sovereignty, it has requirements of governance similar to those of sovereign states. The preservation and growth of the investor's capital, or what might be called the increase of wealth of this lesser polity; the cultivation of excellence appropriate to the tasks at hand and in the future; the requirement of increasing productivity while at the same time retaining the loyalties of and opportunities for employees—these and many similar demands of governance require prudential abilities of a very high order.

Preservation of political liberty is the goal of these aristocratic possibilities sanctioned or created by the Constitution. Citizens are raised to the goal of liberty by the exercise of appropriate powers, the opportunities for which are pervasive. America provides no clear route for any particular class: no privilege of rank, nor state religion, nor national universities. Instead, we depend upon nature, grown luxuriant by prosperity, and upon people, driven by ambition. In this manner the polity nurtures its citizens.

The American polity offers a share of rule to a multitude of gifted persons who are cast up in every generation by liberty and prosperity.

[21] See, for example, Hilary Rose and Steven Rose, "The Rise of Radical Science," *New Scientist*, vol. 84, no. 1188 (Jan. 3, 1980), p. 28.

[22] For a recent discussion of "middle class morality," see Bruno Bettelheim, "Education and the Reality Principle," *American Educator*, vol. 3, no. 4 (Winter 1979), p. 10.

It shapes their opinions and interests so as to make them a part of the oligarchic democracy, a part of the vast and accommodating middle. They are neither democrats simply, nor oligarchs, nor aristocrats. They have the abilities of the best but the opinions of the middle. For this reason they do not see themselves as a separate class, and the tendency toward faction becomes vestigial.

Aristocracy and Democracy

The American republic succeeded in accommodating the natural aristoi. Liberty and prosperity cast them up within the polity because it created a vital place for them. At the same time it molded them in conformity with dominant opinions and interests. This achievement of the American polity, nevertheless, is incomplete and must remain so. The aristoi, by the very principles that permit and encourage them to flourish, cannot be wholly assimilated into the oligarchic character of the American democracy. Government, and science and commerce, cannot completely absorb the moral and intellectual, or political, ambition of the aristoi. Their lives cannot be completed in the life of the polity. There is, therefore, what must be called an unassimilable aristoi, which constitutes a true *faction* in our political life. This, and the consequent danger to the republic, are the subjects of this concluding section.

It is necessary to speak of the ambition of the aristoi. Aristocracy cannot be defined by a vague attachment to some transcendent idea. We miss the essential point if we fail to recognize the central importance of ideas in defining and describing their lives. True aristoi are animated by the working out in thought and action of the idea that possesses them. That is their dominant interest, their dominant ambition. They live a life of cultivated intelligence. Their "work" is based upon thought and the acquisition and use of knowledge. They do not eschew self-interest for they are constantly threatened. No class today is more vulnerable or suffers more from impoverishment. It is the very meaning of a life of cultivated intelligence that to be denied its possibilities is to be destroyed.

The central idea that animates the natural aristocracy of our time is moral autonomy. The basis of this view is that man is by nature "free."[23] It is the idea of human self-sufficiency in which morality no

---

[23] Allan Bloom on Rousseau: "Man's freedom, which seems to be independent of and opposed to moral rule is the sole source of morality. With this discovery Rousseau completes the break with the political teaching of classical antiquity begun by Machiavelli and Hobbes." We should add that man is not merely free

longer is identified with piety and hence no longer is formed by custom and law out of reverence for the past and its divinities. Nor is it bound to the intellectual authority of the past. Indeed, it was the severing of the intellectual ties to the past that legitimated the moral rebellion.

This moral idea has extreme possibilities. It can be theoretical, building a noble edifice of utopian hopes upon the idea of human freedom. This is why it is possible for modern moral opinion to be passionate and even fanatical without being religious. It can also be devastatingly practical, denying to man any pretense of noble illusions and conceding to him only the base passions that possess and are thought to define human nature. It is no accident that the radical left in America and the libertarian right meet on the common ground of moral autonomy. And, of course, this moral idea can become nihilistic.

The conflation of moral passion with intellectual achievement is a distinctive mark of the aristocracy of our time. The idea of moral autonomy contains the utopian desire that mankind might regain its original birthright by the exercise of natural reason or some other capacity still more latent. Moral autonomy is the natural child of the modern doctrine of natural rights. This theory was originally designed to destroy the rule of received moral opinion over political life. Rights are based upon "nature" in some sense and not upon human custom (mores) or upon divine revelation. A government based upon such rights might ensure peace and stability, and the people living under its rule would be free from the sanction that received morality gives to political coercion. Obligation would henceforward be contractual, not "moral" in the old sense.

Although the theory of rights was intended to disestablish a moral government of moral constraints, it, in fact, went far toward establishing the idea of moral autonomy as its new conventional morality, in which the "mores" of the public are not tied necessarily to social constraints. The demand for autonomy is potentially infinite or at least as far-reaching as the desires of the human imagination. Human life, however, consists of necessary restraints on desires, both internal and external. The moral demand for radical autonomy thus is an insistent and incessant counterpoint to the necessity of restraint. Government based upon right thus is petitioned to expand the speci-

to choose between right and wrong—the Biblical view—but free *of* right and wrong, which are products of convention. As Bloom observes, ". . . man is a being who wills, and the capacity to do what he wills is the essence of freedom. Willing is, as such, independent of what is willed." In "Jean-Jacques Rousseau," in Leo Strauss and Joseph Cropsey, eds., *History of Political Philosophy*, 1st ed. (Chicago: Rand McNally, 1963).

ficity of those rights, or to legitimate the morality of radical freedom, by granting rights to every desire to be free of human constraints, whether natural or conventional. The consequence of this is a disturbing paradox.

The moral autonomy that the "nonmoral" state sets free now is turned around and judges the "moral" character of the state. Predictably, it is found wanting. Particularly, it is found to be "undemocratic." Political liberty as the central purpose gradually fades as the people forget the alternative, and "freedom" of an intrinsically unspecifiable and unsatisfiable sort replaces it. Thus a state that guarantees liberty on the foundation of rights finds itself attacked by its own citizens as an enemy of freedom. The tensions implicit in egalitarianism, already the common morality, become exacerbated as the language of rights gradually becomes the whole of the language of morality.

Moral autonomy in a republic must be seen as the successor to the idea of virtue, or excellence. In spite of this, excellence lives on in a subterranean fashion. No intellectual achievement and no passion for the moral life, no matter how conceived, can exist without it. But excellence as such cannot be accorded full recognition because of its inegalitarian essence. It is therefore at odds with moral autonomy which, as a teaching, believes itself to be egalitarian. The consequence is an aristocracy divided within, its aristocratic essence wrestling with its egalitarian political program. On the aristocratic ground of radical freedom ideological or totalitarian democracy then becomes the successor to the idea of a republic.

We thus arrive at difficulties that lie close upon the heart of the American and liberal republic: There is no natural and necessary attachment of a significant and growing portion of its aristoi to the idea of a republic, although they appear to be enfranchised by it and prosper. We must ask why it is that the political liberty and self-government of a republic do not appear to fulfill the aspiration for freedom that is implicit in the idea of moral autonomy.

It is first necessary to be reminded that the enfranchisement of the natural aristoi requires accommodation with the oligarchic democracy. But the antipathy of aristocracy to oligarchy is very ancient. Its basis was the view that the exclusive pursuit of wealth or a life devoted primarily to its preservation, corrupted a man and could only be pursued at the expense of others. Quite simply, commerce could not be called the highest and best human activity and was an impediment to the best life. This thought retains its currency today, but its ancient foundation, the idea of virtue, has become uncongenial, if it has not disappeared. Nevertheless, this ancient antipathy was to some degree shared by the cultivated natural aristoi who were the American Founders. Their achievement may be characterized, therefore, as the triumph of prudential reason over taste. But they were also thoroughly modern men, the liberals of their day, and they also participated in the idea of moral autonomy. The subordination of religion was for them not merely policy, but conviction as well. They lived in a time we now find strange. They could easily reach back in thought to the aristocratic opinions of classical antiquity and its traditions which had formed them, while, at the same time, they prepared the way for the supplanting views they wished to see succeed. When, at last, the wave that carried them forward reached the shore, the energy of the classical opinions was dissipated. The waves that followed were not pulled by the moon of classical antiquity, but by the geological spasms of modernity.

Did the Founders understand the consequences of the new idea when set free from the past? They appear to have placed their faith in the good sense of ordinary men to wish to preserve the customs and conventions that inform moral life. They certainly did not believe that it was the place of the law actually to form moral habits and customs, but only to protect and, to a limited extent compatible with their doctrines, to foster them. They appear not to have anticipated the corrosive effect of the new aristocratic idea on the received morality and on the concession to oligarchy upon which the polity rests.

It was not the ancient antipathy to commerce that has made a significant portion of the natural aristoi unable to accommodate themselves to the liberal polity. To be sure, throughout the nineteenth century and even in our own time there was a criticism of the vulgarity and philistinism of the new commercial wealth. Rather, the modern antipathy to the idea of oligarchial democracy found its roots and began to flourish only after the radical intellectual assault on the very foundations of liberalism emerged. This is now and must forever be associated with the name of Karl Marx, although its true progenitor is probably Rousseau.[24] Marx's arguments were intended to strike at the roots of liberal institutions founded upon the idea of natural rights to property and ownership that underlie oligarchic legitimacy. This critique was made in the name of democratic freedom, but must be identified with the aristocratic idea of moral autonomy.

It was the availability of such a critique, and not necessarily agreement with it, that provided the intellectual ground for animating the moral passions by which aristocracy might continue its quarrel

---

[24] Ibid.

with oligarchy. It provided, latterly, a political education for the aristoi which the American republic, with its principled indifference to the opinions of its citizens, could not. It gave legitimacy to the festering resentment of a disfranchised aristocracy who could no longer rule in the name of virtue and who could share in the rule only by acquiescing in an oligarchic democracy they must despise.

What is the true source of the modern antipathy to the oligarchic democracy? Why does the radical critique of it carry the weight of sympathy even when truth is sufficient to balance the scales? Both a love of virtue and superior taste must be ruled out. They are not the terms of the conflict, for they have no defenders of any political vigor. Rather, the battle is so bitter because it is fought over the birthright.

The birthright is the question of merit, or who shall rule. Here the claims of the aristocracy and of the oligarchy clash because they are so similar.

For the modern oligarchy, or classical economic liberalism, the claim to rule is based upon their being the true benefactors of democracy. Those who gain material rewards and inequalities merit them not only because of their unequal effort and ability, but because the public good is served by an "invisible hand." But insofar as *all* are moved by this hand, everyone is both beneficiary and benefactor. It is both just and necessary, therefore, that the property and interests of all be protected by right and that all share in the opportunity to rule, for only in this way will liberty be protected.

For the modern aristocracy, on the other hand, the case for merit is concealed behind the advocacy of radical freedom and equality. The advocacy of equality is based upon the exploitation and, increasingly, the creation of class resentments. The desire to include all cannot be made without the necessity of separating out some either by confiscating wealth or excluding the "privileged" from access to further advantages. Egalitarianism, therefore, is but a weapon against the inequality of the oligarchic component of the liberal polity and can stem from no love of equality for its own sake. In arguing for the superior "social justice" of radical egalitarianism the aristoi in fact assert their claim or title to rule by virtue of superior thought.[25]

[25] Some readers may wonder why the term "intellectual" is absent from the text and may further wonder whether this term is not synonymous with "natural aristocracy" as advanced here. Taking the testimony of the intellectuals themselves, we do, indeed, seem to be in the presence of a separate social genus. As commonly used, the term signifies a class of persons defined by a life of thought as opposed to one of action. We may recognize in this the ancient distinction between theory and practice. Upon closer examination, however, this distinction does not seem rigorously to define the genus. For we observe that, in general, an intellectual is a person of thought, but one whose thought is practiced for the

This fact, that the argument for social justice is made by a class whose life is defined by its articulation of a governing moral idea, must be given greater weight than the actual merit of the arguments. For, left to themselves, the "people," in whose behalf the battle is waged, might well insist upon the advantages—political and economic—of the oligarchs as a solution to their inequality. This would not be a solution to the grievances of the aristoi, however, since they go far deeper, to the very right of the oligarchical claims. So the aristoi forever preach a lesson that the "people" must purge themselves of the illicit desires of the oligarchs; they must not become "bourgeois." Instead, they must rise above their material desires and build a new society devoid of such false relations among men.

The aristocratic claim to rule is not spread simply by a frontal assault on oligarchy, which, in any event, in an oligarchic democracy means an attack upon the middle class. Rather, it undermines the middle class's self-confidence by imposing its tastes. Not only does the unassimilable aristocracy educate our children—giving it control of classrooms and freedom to publish is one of the chief means by which the ever elastic oligarchic democracy seeks to accommodate this class—it also provides the "culture" and thereby the aspirations of the middle class. In this way an entertainment industry flourishes in which aristocratic nihilism is transformed into gratuitous and gratifying violence, and aristocratic sexual license becomes middle-class pornography. Movements of inner liberation flourish, which offer the middle class "moral" reasons for abandoning frugality, self-restraint, and responsibility, all in the name of freedom.

Why do the aristoi want to corrupt the middle class? Of course, it is not seen as corruption, but as the improvement of middle-class

---

sake of advancing certain kinds of action, and who writes for influential journals of opinion (if possible) with a view to causing or to halting such actions as he may favor or oppose. Such a person's life may be said to be governed and animated by a notion of right action more than—or even to the exclusion of—a life of theory or learning for its own sake. Nevertheless, what distinguishes an intellectual from a journalist is the intellectual's pretension to autonomy and originality of thought as opposed to being derivative.

Moreover, "intellectual" may fairly be called a job description, because it indicates the kind of work—writing of a certain kind for a certain kind of audience for a certain purpose—done, it is to be hoped, for a living, or at least in the absence of economic constraints and political repression.

Intellectuals, as a class, must then be defined as a species—not a genus—of political persons who are possessed by some notion of "the good," who wish to cause action through writing, and who hope to make a living at it or in spite of it. If we then ask to what genus this species belongs, we see that they are members of the natural aristocracy, that is, of that class whose lives are governed by their natural intellectual abilities and by the opinions that animate those abilities. Intellectuals are thus cousins to those from whom they most wish to be distinguished, the captains of industry, the "movers and shakers," and the scientists.

standards and tastes, which are narrow and prejudiced. It is revolutionary rule over the middle class from within in the name of moral autonomy and radical freedom. It is thus a means of exercising revolutionary rule over conventional morality. To achieve this it is necessary to be invulnerable to the charges of immorality. But to have an advanced morality is, indeed, to be "moral" and then some. If, therefore, the morality of the middle class is transformed by identification with that of the aristoi, the latter are held blameless.

The political strategy of the unassimilable aristoi has been to drive a wedge between oligarchy and democracy. But where democracy—what Aristotle would have called an extreme—does not yet exist, because there is in fact an oligarchic democracy, it is first necessary to undermine the self-confidence of the middle class by creating resentments against the polity. But these are projections of the aristocracy's own resentments. For resentment is now the aristocratic passion, not the democratic passion.

This aristocracy allies itself in all the liberal polities with an idea of democracy—not with the existing idea of democracy but with one that would be content with aristocratic rule. This is called socialism. Both its benign and its malignant forms are solutions to the political problem that seek to eliminate the oligarchical element. That is, they seek to eliminate rather than to accommodate the sources of conflict.

Socialism is modern aristocratic democracy. It is meant to supplant oligarchic democracy. Aristocratic and oligarchic democracy both disguise the part that aristocracy plays, primarily because aristocracy no longer understands itself as such. This failure of self-understanding is the source of the tragic character of its political thought. In fact, socialism does not eliminate the oligarchy; this is its myth, just as oligarchic democracy does not eliminate the aristocracy, which is its myth.

In socialism the aristocracy are mentors of democracy and guardians of its purity. At first it appears that the aristocracy rules by a superior justice based upon "science." Tragically, however, it requires totalitarian rule to keep the democracy "pure." Radical socialism, moreover, brings into being the only pure oligarchies on the earth, the party oligarchies. Although they are not initially oligarchical on the basis of wealth, but on the basis of fewness of numbers and the merit of having been "heroes of the revolution," the party oligarchies later enrich themselves and acquire the inequalities and privileges of the few. To do this they must keep the party relatively exclusive, and, by force and ideological persuasion, the democrats are kept "pure" by remaining "proletarianized." The party, after all, controls the military and the means of production. The party oligarchies must also eliminate their opposition. Inevitably there are purges, and the original "heroes of the revolution," or revolutionary aristocrats, perish. Aristocratic democracy thus becomes de facto rule of the privileged few over the impoverished many—with almost no surviving aristocracy.

Such a regime is deceptively stable. Eventually the natural aristoi reemerge in order to serve the state through expertise. A few inevitably will nourish the aristocratic ambition to rule on the basis of a superior justice, derived from a study of the inferior justice of the ruling oligarchy. They might well rediscover their natural affinity for republicanism and the rule of law, as have many Soviet dissidents. But from this rediscovery in thought, to the actual founding of a republic, requires knowledge of a route thus far traversed successfully by no one and unmarked on any map.

Afterword: Party and Faction

We have argued in this essay that the major American political parties are not identical with the elements of faction that are potentially or actually present in the United States. The elements of faction, properly understood, we have argued, are democracy, oligarchy, and aristocracy. Only the last named, or a portion of it, may be considered unassimilable within or standing outside of the American political solution. It is now necessary to speculate about the consequences for the larger polity of this relatively small, but disproportionately potent, faction.

Were the political parties to unravel—a process now said to be underway—would they be succeeded by true political dissension, that is, the reemergence of fatal faction? Such a sequence of events is not necessary. Still, it is thinkable, and the speculation must be pursued.

The most deadly factions that could emerge would be those of a peculiarly American version of the poor versus the rich. A quarrel of this kind, however, not only means an impoverishment and shrinking of the middle class—this has occurred in the past, after all—but as well the undermining of the self-confidence of the middle class in such a way as to change its attachment to the polity.

As the aristocratic opinions undermine the moral conventions of the middle class, the aristocratic faction becomes the catalyst for the moral uncertainty of the middle class. A prideful condition of the middle class evolves—imitating the *hubris* of the aristoi—combining a conviction of infinite worth and unlimited possibilities. This pride is hollow, however, because it is equivalent to moral uncertainty, as it offers no certain guide to action, but only to reaction. As economic conditions deteriorate—itself a consequence of legislation reflecting the changed moral condition—the middle-class "interest" becomes the protection of the *idea* of moral autonomy, or radical freedom. The economic expression of this interest is a growing sense of entitlement to the material condition of prosperity and security. There is a subtle but crucial difference between this view and that of protecting one's own—and everyone's—self-interest and right to property for the sake of political liberty. The growing erosion of material conditions naturally breeds a resentment of inequalities. Middle-class populism increases in strength, a corollary of which is the dismantling of the traditional structures of the political parties. This populism distrusts representative government, and there is a popular outcry for direct democracy, that is, for the extreme idea of democratic office. The representatives cannot long resist these passions, and the judiciary already "legislates" in its behalf. There is a clamor for federal protection of a notion of "human rights"—reflected in the nation's foreign policy as well—to human fulfillment or full humanity and dignity, which, in fact, is a desire for freedom from all constraints. The demand for new rights—to a job, a house, medical care, dignity, etc.—reflects the desire to protect one's sense of autonomy against a deep-seated moral insecurity, that is, a moral inability to deal with the uncertainty that a conviction of unlimited natural freedom breeds. In practice this means not equal opportunity or access for all, but the exclusion of some. This universal "affirmative action" is, in fact, the seed of faction. Inevitably, this results in an erosion of the rights of property in the name of equality, because the federal "guarantee" can be underwritten only by the confiscation of the wealth of some. This, in turn, is the beginning of the end to all civil, that is, political, liberties.[26]

There are aristoi who defend political liberty against radical freedom and equality, but only with difficulty. The prudential case appears strong because the consequences for political liberty under a regime of radical equality are painfully apparent. Nevertheless, the prudential case is less than persuasive. The defense of the middle class does not come easily to the aristocracy. The reason is that the

[26] See Stephen Miller, "Human Rights in Foreign Policy: A Soviet Success," *The American Spectator* (January 1980), p. 11: "According to Kenneth Minogue, whose essay 'The History of the Idea of Human Rights' appears in *The Human Rights Reader*, Locke implies that 'everyone has a property in his own person.' . . . The citizen thus protects himself from the state not only by owning property, but also by being himself a kind of property—something that the state cannot trespass against. In their defense of property and civil rights, the Founding Fathers were descendents of Locke. 'Every man,' Madison said, had a 'right to his property' and 'a property in his rights.'"

idea that unites the aristoi—moral autonomy—may be stronger than what divides them.

Is it both desirable and possible to break the grip of this idea and, if so, on what intellectual basis? Is this the central political-philosophical question of our time?

6

Political Change and Party Reform

James W. Ceaser

Three important groups in this century have consciously adopted the label of reformers: the Progressives, the advocates of responsible political parties, and the proponents of an open presidential selection process. Despite significant differences among the three, they share enough common ground to make it reasonable to refer to them by the same name. Specifically, all have espoused the following three general views.

First, they have criticized the traditional pluralistic element of American politics that sanctions quiet accommodation among groups and tolerates participation based on self-interest. Reformers have used this criticism as their most visible rallying point, no doubt because it taps a moral theme that can easily be employed to discredit the status quo. Reform rhetoric has been filled from the first with a Manichean dualism that pits, in the Progressives' language, the "darkness" of the existing system against the "light" of a reformed system or, in the words of recent reformers, the "old" against the "new" politics. Reformers have attempted to replace self-interest as a motive for participation with new and more enlightened motives—with a commitment to serve the public good in a transpartisan fashion (the Progressive vision), with a dedication to one or another of two fundamental political principles (the responsible parties' position), or with a deep concern for the "hard" issues of the day (the goal of recent party reformers).

Second, all three reform groups have called for more democracy. Innovations such as primaries, rule by popular mandate, and initiative and recall have all been proposed under the reform impulse. Reformers have sometimes been confused over exactly what they mean by democracy, as in the most recent case of whether an "open" presidential selection process requires more primaries or only reformed caucuses. Such confusion has, however, been something reformers could tolerate or ignore, at least while they were outsiders attempting to overturn the old system: whatever exactly it was they wanted, reformers felt certain that it would be more democratic than the existing system.

Finally, all three reform movements have sought to endow the American system with a much greater capacity to "respond" and to effect rapid and fundamental changes in policies and laws. Of the shared themes, this last is perhaps the least conspicuous, though probably the most important. Over the course of reform thought in this century, one finds that the dominant substantive concern has been to reverse the alleged bias in our system for inaction and to replace it with a bias that favors change and new initiatives. In a sense, this objective is the end for which the other two reform goals have been the means. Reformers have attacked pluralism as an impediment to responsiveness and have held up democracy as the value that can justify making rapid changes.

The Progressive attack on the immobilism of the traditional system was given its classic expression by Woodrow Wilson. Wilson argued that the formal constitutional system was built on Newtonian principles that were designed to create a static equilibrium. The political parties that grew up within this system reflected its basic conservatism and evolved into heterogeneous bodies which, for fear of losing their traditional support, preferred to cling to old principles and platitudes. Responsible party advocates and recent reformers have echoed this criticism, claiming that the traditional system produces "delay and devitalization" and precludes an open discussion of the vital issues facing society.[1]

To overcome this immobilism, reformers have proposed changes in the electoral system and in the arrangement and powers of the formal institutions. In the case of the Progressives, the general objective was to establish a dynamic point of leadership within the regime. At the formal institutional level, this took the form of a call for a greatly expanded role for the president, conceived now as a popular spokesman for the national community. At the electoral level, it centered on a plan to choose presidential nominees by national primaries, a proposal designed to serve the dual purposes of destroying the old parties and opening the nomination process to aspirants who could raise new issues and build popular support for them. Advocates of responsible parties called for a de facto end to the

[1] James MacGregor Burns, *The Deadlock of Democracy* (Englewood Cliffs, N.J.: Prentice-Hall, 1963), p. 5.

separation of powers, to be brought about by establishing disciplined, programmatic parties connecting the executive with the legislative branch. The existence of a clear choice between parties at elections would give the victorious party a mandate to implement its proposals. Finally, recent reformers have relied entirely on a transformation of parties to endow the system with a greater capacity for change and have avoided any systematic proposals for altering the basic institutional relationship between the president and Congress. Although the recent reformers have been the only reform group to base their case exclusively on a change in the selection process, all reformers have accorded a prominent place to the presidential selection process, viewing it as one of the best points of entrée in the system for new initiatives.

In this essay I analyze the connection between perspectives on political change and the arrangement of our institutions, giving particular emphasis to the role of the electoral process. Specifically, I address the following three questions: (1) What, briefly, were the major prereform perspectives on political change? (2) What views of political change were embodied in the debate between responsible-party advocates and the consensual school in the 1950s and 1960s? and (3) How do empirical findings on critical elections bear on this debate? I then make a case for the superiority of a modified consensual position and conclude by discussing what changes in our electoral process, if any, could institutionalize the values of this position.

Prereform Perspectives on Political Change

Every viable political system must have the capacity to "renew" itself by making fundamental changes in policy in response to new demands or new circumstances. This statement is admittedly vague, but most can readily grasp its meaning. In the United States, our political system has had to adapt to such demands as ending slavery, building a welfare state, and assuming a leading role in international affairs. In all serious discussions of constitutional design, the question of the political system's capacity to adopt significant change inevitably occupies a central place.

As noted, one of the major criticisms of the Founding Fathers in this century is that they failed to provide adequately for change. This charge contains a substantial degree of validity, although it has usually been exaggerated and attended by a failure to acknowledge much of what the Founders did say about political change. The critique of the Founders' views, if subject to close analysis, consists of two points, one relating to their understanding of the scope of necessary change and the other to their view of the method by which change should be effected.

On the first count, it is by now well established that the Founders wanted to avoid anything resembling intense conflict among national political parties.[2] Such conflict, they held, could easily degenerate into "great" conflict over first principles of religion, politics, or property, such as rich versus poor. Religious differences, they thought, could be kept out of politics by the principle of separation of church and state; fundamental political differences by a general acceptance of the Constitution and the republican form of government; and basic property disputes by emphasizing a struggle among numerous minor parties or interest groups that would substitute for—and sap the energy of—a more intense class division. Along with these general solutions, the Founders offered the institutional device of a nonpartisan presidential selection process that would focus on candidate character and incumbent performance as the criteria for choice. This method of selection would serve to keep issues from becoming part of the struggle for the nation's highest office, thus avoiding the possibility that presidential contests would generate "great" conflicts.

While the Founders never envisaged an absence of conflict within the councils of the government, it is fair to say that they either did not anticipate or saw no institutional means of providing for great divisions that systematically involved the public. Their perceptions were not entirely unrealistic. The fact is that for most of our history their expectations have been met. Even the existence of partisan conflict does not controvert this statement, for as both the critics and defenders of our traditional party system maintain, party conflict has usually involved disputes over secondary issues. Still, there have been exceptions, times at which conflict has assumed a more fundamental character than the Founders ever expected. As Madison saw soon after the establishment of the Constitution, and as Lincoln and Franklin Roosevelt both realized, "great" conflict did not come to an end in 1787.

In the Founders' view, the best way to effect change was through initiation from the "top," that is, from Congress acting as a deliberative body and especially from the president. The natural tendency of the highest kind of politician, the Founders believed, would be to leave behind a record of distinction, which could best be obtained by launching bold projects and new initiatives. Of course, the Founders did not

[2] See Richard Hofstadter, *The Idea of a Party System* (Berkeley: University of California Press, 1972), pp. 1-74, and my own *Presidential Selection* (Princeton, N.J.: Princeton University Press, 1979), pp. 41-122.

regard all pressure from the "bottom," that is, from public opinion, as undesirable. They clearly thought that what the public wanted should be represented and taken into account, though they did not believe that public opinion should—or could—govern. In addition, the Founders held that presidential elections had a legitimate role to play in stimulating change. As Hamilton makes clear, a negative popular judgment on the performance of an incumbent would serve as a signal for his successor to embark on a different set of policies.[3] In the main, however, the Founders held that the initiative for change should derive from elected officials acting free from immediate popular constraints, and much of their effort in designing the Constitution was directed at providing a realm of discretion for elected officials.

Although this view may now appear antiquarian and undemocratic, it is not entirely undescriptive of how fundamental change has actually been initiated. Contrary to the impression left by many students of electoral politics, the impetus for new departures has not always derived from parties or public opinion, but has come from the top, often from presidents employing their best judgment and looking for renown. Nevertheless, as in the case of the Founders' understanding of the scope of change, their twentieth-century critics have a point. To understand fully the operation of the American political system, we must acknowledge that through the instrument of political parties the nation has developed a supplementary source for change and renewal that the Founders did not contemplate; and it would be difficult now to conceive of our system operating without this new institutional capacity.

In itself, the founding of parties in the 1790s did not mark a decisive shift in the dominant theory of political change, whatever it might have accomplished in practice. As Richard Hofstadter has shown, neither the Jeffersonians nor the Federalists looked on party competition as a permanent feature of American politics; instead, both regarded parties as temporary or "emergency" agencies to rescue the system from a potentially seditious foe, after which the regime could be reestablished on its proper nonpartisan foundation.[4]

The true founder of the idea of permanent party competition was not Jefferson or Hamilton, but Martin Van Buren. Van Buren's original objective, however, had little in common with the reform view of political change. In fact, his views on change were much closer to the Founders, despite their preference for nonpartisanship, than to con-

[3] Alexander Hamilton, James Madison, and John Jay, *The Federalist Papers*, ed. Clinton Rossiter (New York: New American Library, 1961), No. 72, p. 436.

[4] Hofstadter, *The Idea*, pp. 41-74.

temporary reformers who profess a belief in strong party competition. Van Buren proposed party competition for the express purpose of encouraging moderation and avoiding the possibility of dangerous pressure from outside the government. His views on the national electoral process crystallized during the election of 1824, after he had had a chance to observe the problems with an open and democratic nonpartisan system. (This system was quite different from the one the Founders had intended, for even though it had no parties, it was based on the candidates' attempts to rouse the people by issue or personality appeals.) In Van Buren's view, this kind of system opened the way to personal factionalism in which numerous aspirants, driven by their ambition to become president, might engage in demagogy or fan dangerous divisions. If ambition was a potentially constructive force within the presidency, it was, according to Van Buren, a dangerous force when left unregulated in the pursuit of that office. To solve this problem, he proposed permanent competition between two stable and moderate parties controlled by seasoned politicians. These parties would restrain presidential aspirants, inducing them to take moderate positions.

With Van Buren, then, we find a clear recognition of the necessity and legitimacy of direct pressure from "below" the formal institutions, yet at the same time an attempt to control the character of that pressure. Van Buren viewed the parties, in a sense, as parts of the institutional system rather than as instruments formed to win power to effect major change. His "institutional" perspective on parties may therefore be contrasted with a "partisan" perspective, according to which the stand a particular party takes is more important than maintaining the "institution" of stable two-party competition. The difference between these perspectives is well illustrated in the following two statements, the first from Van Buren (in 1827) and the second from Lincoln (in 1858):

> If the old ones [party feelings] are suppressed, geographical divisions founded on local interests or, what is worse, prejudices between free and slaveholding states will inevitably take their place. Party attachment in former times furnished a complete antidote for sectional prejudices by producing counteracting feelings.[5]

> A House divided against itself cannot stand. I believe this government cannot endure permanently half slave and half

[5] Letter to Thomas Ritchie, January 13, 1827, cited in Arthur Schlesinger, Jr., ed., *History of American Presidential Elections*, vol. 1 (New York: Chelsea House, 1973), pp. 618-19.

> free. . . . Our cause, then, must be entrusted to, and conducted by, its own undoubted friends—those whose hands are free, whose hearts are in the work—who do care for the results.[6]

This statement of a dichotomy between these perspectives cannot be considered the last word on the nineteenth-century view of political change. Despite the tension between these positions, they both exist (and have existed) within the same institutional framework. Van Buren in effect prepared the way for this compromise. By making party competition legitimate and by permitting challenges from minor parties (notwithstanding his preference for stable major parties), Van Buren allowed for the possibility of occasional "partisan" uses of parties and thus for the possibility of change deriving from an electoral organization. The "partisan" use of parties, while exceptional under Van Buren's system, was nonetheless permissible. Van Buren himself accepted this amendment to his earlier views when, faced with the situation of his own party's failure to limit slavery, he took the extraordinary step of leading one of the nation's first third-party challenges in 1848.

Thus the final prereform position on the relationship between the electoral process and political change can be stated as follows. Normally, the electoral system should work to prevent major pressure for change from translating itself too quickly into party policy. This bias is built into the system in the belief that an open system removes restraints on presidential aspirants and encourages them to appeal to dangerous and immoderate currents of opinion. Yet the moderation of the existing parties itself needs a check; occasional demands for change and renewal must be accommodated. These objectives can be accomplished by permitting a new party to be created or an old one to be reconstituted. Under this method, change takes place when a party sets forth a new program in response to some particular substantive problem and then attempts to win the political power to enact it. There is no need, accordingly, to alter the character of electoral institutions or explicitly change the permanent distribution of power among the formal institutions.

This method for effecting change contrasts directly with the reform idea. According to reformers, the way to ensure an adequate capacity for change is to restructure the electoral process and sometimes the entire political system as well. The problem in the regime,

[6] Speech at Springfield, June 16, 1858, cited in Robert W. Johannsen, ed., *The Lincoln-Douglas Debates* (New York: Oxford University Press, 1965), pp. 14-21.

as reformers see it, is less with any particular crisis the nation faces, such as the need for welfare measures or the Vietnam war, than with a general, systemic incapacity to adapt. Particular crises are seen as the inevitable manifestations of this underlying problem, in this view. Accordingly, it is only by permanent alterations in our institutional structures that the real defects of our political system can be overcome. Whether this additional impetus for change is necessary, or whether it incurs too great a risk by opening the way to demagogic politics and false renewals, is the question that has been at the heart of the dispute between reformers and their opponents throughout this century.

Recent Perspectives on Political Change

The question of the relationship between the electoral process and the system's capacity for change entered the mainstream of political science in the debate in the 1950s and 1960s between responsible-party advocates and defenders of the existing party system.[7] The latter, members of what I call the consensual school, based their defense of the traditional party system on the following points:

1. It moderated political conflict and helped promote consensus.
2. It discouraged demagogic appeals by presidential aspirants both before the nomination, by minimizing the need to engage in direct popular appeals, and afterward, by holding the candidates to the moderate position staked out by the party.
3. It did not fundamentally alter the basic operation of the original constitutional system, and such alterations as it did introduce were generally salutary. Thus, in the way of minor alterations, the party system imposed some kind of restraint on the executive by making the president answerable to an identifiable constituency (the major party leaders) that had some say over his renomination; in return, the party gave the president a guarantee of some degree of popular support for his policies, the likelihood of renomination, and a modicum of coordination with the congressional wing of the party. For all this, however, the system was not changed at its foundations: presidents were not bound to an ideological program that undermined their discretion; and congressmen could still break with a president of the same party to represent local interests or defend the prerogatives of their institution. In short, party government never replaced constitutional government.

[7] For statements of these two views, see Robert A. Goldwin, ed., *Political Parties, U.S.A.* (Chicago: Rand McNally, 1961).

4. It provided a modest kind of responsibility. Whatever the reality of the notion of collective responsibility, voters perceived enough of it to punish a party for the poor performance of an incumbent. The opportunity to exercise this sanction filled an important "psychological" need of the electorate to have someone or something take the blame for a bad turn of events, thus leaving the people in an optimistic frame of mind. It was precisely the moderate character of the choice offered between the parties that allowed voters to exercise this option. Voters could safely deviate from their normal partisan allegiance because the opposition party was not viewed as too extreme or radical.

Responsible-party advocates, on the other hand, attacked the moderate, consensual bias of the existing party system. They called instead for competition between two truly strong parties, meaning parties that were organized not only to elect persons to office but also to enact their programs once in power. The two basic structural changes sought by party government advocates were, first, to eliminate the old sources of power within the parties, which were held by party politicians concerned with maintaining state and local organizations, and replace them with new kinds of organizations in which party members would be directly concerned with national issues; and second, to transform all federal elections, congressional as well as presidential, into referenda on the platforms and performance of the national parties. In the deepest sense, the objective of the party government school was to change the political system as a whole, substituting the party government principle of simple majority rule for the more complex system established by the Founders. According to party government advocates, the principal check on potential abuses of power would now come not from a separation of powers but from popular elections. Nor was there any reason to fear a factional majority, for, according to James MacGregor Burns, a national "popular majority, like democratic politics in general, furnishes its own checks and balances."[8] Contrary to the consensual school's position that safe national majorities were the product of a particular institutional arrangement, party government advocates claimed that responsible (but not moderate) parties automatically resulted from the process of forming a majority.

The establishment of party government, according to its proponents, would create a totally responsible government. Voters would

[8] James MacGregor Burns, *Congress on Trial* (New York: Harper and Row, 1949), p. 39.

know exactly where to place blame and could choose the programmatic direction in which they wanted to see the nation move. A second benefit proponents saw was that party government would reverse the presumption in our political system from inaction to action. National elections would present clear choices on present issues, and, once elected, a party would have the power to enact its program without delay.

It is less a criticism than a frank recognition of the facts to say that the entire party government doctrine was a thinly veiled "partisan" instrument of welfare state liberalism. When party government advocates spoke of the complacency of the existing system and the need for change, it was in light of their preference, in nearly all cases, for a vast expansion in the level of federal expenditures. Of course a conservative party was envisaged as the opponent of a liberal party, but the clear assumption was that the conservative cause would fare less well under the new system. It would lose its support in the institutions of the regime and be forced to take its case directly before the bar of public opinion. If liberals today are somewhat less fascinated by the idea of full-blown party government, it is probably because they are now the beneficiaries of a good many institutional features in our system that aid the cause of liberalism, often in defiance of public opinion.

Just as the debate on party structure was reaching its high point in the early 1960s, political scientists began to lose interest in it. The focus in the study of electoral politics shifted from party structure to voting behavior, and few made any systematic effort to connect the two. This development is especially surprising given the findings of the historical inquiry into voting patterns, for they seem to speak directly to the issues of the structural debate. Students of past voting behavior documented quite clearly the periodic recurrence of critical elections in which large numbers of voters shifted party allegiance or in which new voters gave their allegiance disproportionately to one of the parties. These election sets—1796–1800, 1832, 1856–1860, and 1932–1936—were characterized by unusual intensity (by American standards) and presented the electorate with rather clear policy choices, allowing for the potential at times for significant change.

What is crucial to observe at this point is that these choices took place under electoral systems that did not meet the structural requirements of the party government school. On the contrary, after 1828, they occurred under the very selection system that party government advocates condemned. Of course the parties at these moments did not always behave in exactly the moderate way that some consensualists advocated. But the crucial point is that the institutional framework favored by the consensual school has not been impervious to parties that offer significant choices. When the pressure is great enough, or when the situation demands, a new party or a re-invigorated old party can break through the barriers that promote consensus to present an option for significant change.

Critical elections theorists, as I noted, have given only scant attention to the implications of their own findings for the debate on party structure. One line of argument, suggested by James Sundquist, is that the discovery of critical realignments makes the entire structural debate meaningless. The reason is that history—meaning the conflicts thrown up from society over the course of time—determines the conflict situation. History is the independent variable; the degree of choice parties offer is the dependent variable. To quote Sundquist: "To admonish the parties against polarization, or to suggest that it is the *party system* that has become 'unhealthy' if polarization occurs, is to put the blame in the wrong place. . . . When a society polarizes, so do the parties." But no sooner does Sundquist make this argument than he qualifies it, conceding that how the party system is arranged does make a difference: "If moderation, centrism, and compromise are the signs of party health, then virtually everything the country has been doing in the way of institutional reform in the past seventy-five years has worked against this end."[9]

Accepting this last view, we can say that there are two variables that affect the choice that parties offer—history and structure. An approach to the study of parties that excludes either is inadequate. Each independently influences the degree of choice, and in fact the two probably cannot be disentangled, as history does not move in isolation from the institutions of society. Thus if the determinative influence of party structure on choice is less than was often assumed in the original debate between the consensual and party government schools, it is still far from insignificant. This makes the old debate relevant today, although the findings of critical realignment scholars demand that the terms of that debate be restated.

The "new" consensual position can be restated as follows: the best party system is one that encourages the establishment of moderate parties and in so doing creates an institutional presumption against major proposals for change that are not immediately endorsed by one of the major parties. This system should not, however, be closed altogether to the possibility of change, as the major parties can become

[9] James Sundquist, *Dynamics of the Party System* (Washington, D.C.: The Brookings Institution, 1973), pp. 304, 307.

stagnant and lose touch with vital movements within society. A proper check on the major parties is provided by an open electoral system which allows new parties to form. The bias against change remains, and such major renewals as we have must establish themselves against the natural grain of the system. This position, obviously, is a restatement of the view that evolved in the nineteenth century.

The position of the choice school must also be reconstructed. It can no longer contend that we never get choice, but must instead argue that we do not get enough choice enough of the time. Indeed, Walter Dean Burnham, who appears to favor much greater choice in our elections, has argued something very close to this: "Critical realignments are evidence not of the presence of linkages or conditions in the normal state of American politics, but precisely of their absence. Correspondingly they are not manifestations of democratic accountability, but infrequent and hazardous substitutes for it."[10] Paradoxically, then, the position of the choice school boils down to the argument that under the consensual system we get *too much* choice and change at certain elections, and that if we had more choice on a regular basis we could avoid the problems that give rise to these dangerous contests.

The restatement of these two views, I would argue, leaves the consensus school in a much stronger position. Not only does the institutional arrangement it supports allow for significant change, but also there is no intuitive reason for supposing that we need fundamental change more than once every generation. The existence of elections in between these periods may serve an altogether different (and necessary) function: replacing or turning out leaders who have become stale, who have mismanaged the running of the government, or who have made serious errors of judgment. The more telling argument in deciding between these two views derives not from the strength of the consensual school's position, but from the weakness of the choice school's position, which rests in the final analysis on a striking combination of bold exaggeration and bald assertion.

Its first substantive point, that critical elections pose choices that threaten the system, does not square with historical evidence except in the case of 1860. Certainly, the other elections in question—1832, 1896, and 1936—were spirited affairs in which the lines of conflict were clearly drawn. In no sense, however, was the regime threatened because of the positions taken by the parties at these elections; on the contrary, the major parties probably did a great deal to moderate the potential conflict. The second point, that the problems that led to

[10] Walter Dean Burnham, "The End of Party Politics," *TransAction*, vol. 7, no. 2, (Dec. 1969).

these critical elections could have been solved in advance by programmatic parties, has no foundation. It may sound very appealing to say that we could have solved the slavery problem in the 1850s, stopped mortgage foreclosures on farms in the 1890s, and avoided the Great Depression in the 1930s, but is there anything more than mere assertion in these claims? Have any solid arguments been presented that would lead one to believe that programmatic parties could have arisen that were able both to win power and to deal with these problems with the requisite knowledge and foresight? Just as easily might one argue that we could have dealt with all these problems in advance if only we had had philosopher kings as presidents.

Perhaps the point that no one in the choice school wants to admit is that many of the crises our nation has experienced could not have been foreseen by rulers of reasonable intelligence nor, even if foreseen, solved within the constraints of a democratic polity. This is not to say that there could not, somehow, have been better or wiser decisions. But it is to say that there may not have been any *institutional* change that could have guaranteed such decisions. It is an affliction of one strain in the American mindset that when something goes wrong, some cannot attribute it to unavoidable circumstance or normal human failing, but must instead see it as remediable by some institutional change. More than anything else, it may be the inability to accept the inevitable limitations of politics that lies at the basis of reformist thought.

The Party System and Political Change in the Future

The context of the present debate on parties is quite different from that of two decades ago. Then, the responsible-party advocates talked about replacing the existing parties, which by today's standards would be considered strong and viable, with stronger parties still. Today, there is almost universal agreement that our national parties are mere shadows of what they once were. With the great increase in the number of presidential primaries that has occurred since 1968, the current system has evolved into an essentially plebiscitary process in which the individual aspirants stand "above" the party and seek to define its content. The "open" system at the nominating stage now very much resembles the popular nonpartisan system at the final election stage that Van Buren attacked in 1824.

Ironically, remnants of both the consensual and party government schools agree on many of their complaints about the weakness of the current parties, though beneath the surface their final goals remain as different as before. Consensualists lament the demise of the old parties, while party government advocates seek to build responsible parties atop the ruins of the old system. Even contemporary reformers, who did so much to bring down the old system, have not been altogether pleased with the results. Some maintain that their intent was not to establish a system dominated by primaries, but rather only to reform organizational procedures and transfer power from the old regulars to a new group of issue-oriented individuals.

One would think that the new system is sufficiently open to new initiatives to satisfy the reformers. Yet here, too, there have been some second thoughts. Reformers have wondered on the one hand whether the system is not too open to the wrong kind of changes (a concern widely voiced in 1975 in response to George Wallace's candidacy), and on the other hand whether it is too susceptible to soft, image appeals that muffle demands for change and avoid the real issues (a concern that was frequently expressed in the aftermath of Carter's unexpected success in 1976).

Virtually all schools of thought, accordingly, favor strengthening parties in some way. Yet if one is to be at all practical in considering changes in the electoral process, one needs more than expressions of preference. One must also consider what kind of changes are possible and what the results of any proposed change are likely to be. Because the question of what is possible could be debated endlessly, the most I will do here is state what I conceive to be a reasonable position. I will assume that we cannot alter most longstanding structural features that affect the party system (like Civil Service reform) or change basic political styles that derive from major sociological transformations (like the "amateur" impulse for participation associated with the growth of the upper middle class); but that we could make a significant change in the way leaders think about the electoral process and that we therefore could modify or abolish any of the recently adopted party rules or laws affecting the electoral process. I am assuming, in other words, that we still have it within our power to reform the reforms. Admittedly, this may exaggerate our actual degree of choice, but my criterion of "possibility" is meant to be less strenuous than probability.

Even if we had this rather broad range of choice, the problem remains of what to do. Suppose we wanted to reestablish the values of consensus and moderation that were promoted under the prereform selection system. The logical plan, one would think, would be to restore some of the previous prerogatives to the party organizations. But, under present conditions, is there any assurance that this plan would serve the intended purpose?

For some time now American politics has been witnessing a steady increase in organizational participation by "amateurs." The amateur, as defined by James Q. Wilson, is one who participates in politics chiefly to realize certain policy goals, rather than for material reward (like a job) or solidary satisfaction (socializing with others).[11] Amateurs have always played a role in American politics, of course, and there were moments in the past, associated with critical elections, in which they exercised great influence in party affairs. But today, because of Civil Service reform and a general rise in affluence and educational levels, there is good reason to believe that any kind of restored party organizations would normally be strongly influenced, and probably dominated, by amateurs. Parties in the future would therefore not look like they did in the past and might not perform the same functions. In fact, if one is honest about what political science can tell us today, one has to admit that we are probably more in the dark about the consequences of institutional changes in the electoral process than at any time since the 1820s. All one can do, therefore, is cite the possible outcomes, offer some informed guesses as to which is most likely, and make proposals that take into account the fact of uncertainty.

The first possibility is that the new parties would be highly ideological and would attempt, to a degree never seen in American politics, to dictate policy to elected officials. The evidence supporting this conclusion derives from an impressive body of research on amateurs, all of which indicates that they tend to be ideologically inclined and ill-disposed toward compromise. They prefer purity to victory, though they would like both.[12] Thus, far from producing moderation, a move to restore power to party organizations might well force an unwanted extremism on the American electorate.

If this is the most likely outcome, then those favoring moderation would probably find themselves in the curious position of supporting a plebiscitary system over a system of strong parties. In a striking reversal of every traditional account of parties since the 1820s, moderates would have to brand parties as instruments of polarization rather than of consensus, and they would be forced to appeal to the "moderation" of the people against the extremism of the parties. This is no mere textbook possibility. Between 1972 and 1976 there were

[11] James Q. Wilson, *Political Organizations* (New York: Basic Books, 1973).

[12] For two recent empirical accounts of the role of amateurs in national politics, see Denis Sullivan, Jeffrey Pressman, Benjamin Page, and John Lyons, *The Politics of Representation* (New York: St. Martin's Press, 1974); and Denis Sullivan, Jeffrey Pressman, and F. Christopher Arterton, *Explorations in Convention Decisionmaking* (San Francisco: W. H. Freeman, 1972).

instances in which moderates in the Democratic party supported primaries out of fear that ideological activists would dominate non-primary procedures.[13]

A second possibility is that parties would be instruments of relative moderation, even if they would never quite regain the flexibility of our previous parties. According to this view, there is little danger that any kind of party in the American system could dictate policy to elected officials. The Constitution itself, with the formal powers it bestows on its officers and with the separation of powers it specifies, makes anything like party government impossible. Because the American system is much more a product of the formal Constitution than of any informal adaptations (like the party system), any alteration as major as party government would require a constitutional amendment. What then about the degree of conflict that the parties might create and the positions of the candidates that they would nominate?

Here, proponents of the view that parties would be relatively moderate have two rejoinders to their opponents. In the first place, while amateurs might well become the dominant force within the party, they will be far from totally displacing more traditional regulars. Many state and local party organizations retain strong elements of "traditional" patronage and solidary politics, a fact that may have been temporarily obscured in the highly ideological climate of the past decade. While no one would maintain that old-style machine politicians could run the national party, one might well see working alliances between some of the more traditional elements of the party and the most moderate amateurs. Second, most research on the behavior of amateurs took place when they were fighting for control of the party with previously entrenched regulars. Part of their penchant for purism might have been a function of their being outsiders in that struggle. Once they become powers within the parties and must accept responsibility for their fate, they may well begin to moderate. There is probably at least something to the view that yesterday's amateur is tomorrow's professional.

Anyone inclined to accept this second model of the character of future parties would be unwise to consider it a certainty. Accordingly, it would make sense to incorporate into any future party system a check on the danger of a party extremism. That check, it may be

---

[13] See Donald M. Fraser, "Democratizing the Democratic Party," in this volume, and Paul David and James Ceaser, *Proportional Representation in Presidential Nominating Politics* (Charlottesville, Va.: University of Virginia Press, 1980), chaps. 1-3.

suggested, would be provided through the market of party competition in a legally open electoral system. In the past, minor parties performed the role of forcing more radical ideas on the major parties. In the future, they might still perform this role, but if parties tend toward the danger suggested above, then the salutary role of third parties (or the threat to form one) might be quite the reverse: serving as potential center forces to keep the major parties from going too far toward the extremes.

To say that we should have an open electoral system is not the same as saying that we should encourage minor parties. That, indeed, would defeat the very benefit of moderation that derives from a "normally" functioning two-party system. Still, minor parties are an important component in maintaining a healthy two-party system, and what needs to be stressed today is the protection of the rights of minor parties. The reason is that in reform thought, the open party has more or less been offered as a substitute for, rather than a supplement to, an open electoral system. Third and fourth party activity has been characterized as being somehow outside the system. Indeed, one of the main arguments used to support the idea of open parties was that parties, as virtual parts of our official electoral process, must represent fairly each and every group and current of opinion. This attitude of "official" incorporation has carried over to the legal sphere, where campaign finance legislation comes quite close to recognizing and institutionalizing the current Democratic and Republican parties.

In the long run, it is clear that the true ally of strong parties—which is to say closed parties—is an open electoral system. Reformers like James Sundquist would be quite right in demanding open parties if (as they say) people whose views do not quite fit in with the major parties "find [that] the political system is closed to them."[14] But this holds only if one identifies the two-party system with the political system. The alternative view is to put some distance between the parties and the official legal system and to have the official legal system adopt a posture of neutrality toward the parties. It then becomes not only plausible, but quite legitimate for members of a particular party to close their doors on some, inviting them (if they wish) to form their own party. A party can only have a degree of tautness and integrity if it can exclude as well as include. A party worthy of the name is not a neutral representative body, but a body that espouses a distinct, even if highly general, viewpoint.

[14] Sundquist, *Dynamics*, p. 307.

The direction, then, that I would suggest for reform is the reverse of much of what we have seen over the past decade. Instead of opening our parties to direct democracy and closing the electoral system, we should be closing our parties and keeping open the electoral system. The existing parties should be strengthened at the same time that the possibility for new parties to emerge is legally protected. Accordingly, as starting points for a new round of reform, I would make two suggestions.

I would ask the national parties and the states to reduce dramatically the number of presidential primaries. If the states are unwilling to do this on their own initiative, as now seems to be the case, the national parties should begin to make efforts to persuade them of the wisdom of this change. In particular, reformers in the Democratic party (who bear much of the responsibility for legitimizing the concept of direct democracy in presidential selection) must be prepared to take the lead. It will not be enough for them merely to call for fewer primaries (as some of them are now doing); they must also be willing to state the grounds on which their new stand is based, which will entail defending the prerogatives of party against the principle of direct democracy. Although one hesitates to ask the national parties to write more rules to reform state procedures—since it was reform of this sort that led the states to adopt primaries in the first place—it may now be that national party "legislation" is the only way to accomplish this goal. What the national parties might consider is a set number of primaries (say, ten) that would be chosen from the willing states on a rotating or a lottery basis.

Second, I would ask the Congress to reconsider existing campaign finance legislation with a view not only to its implications for equitable fund raising, but also to its effects on the well-being of our major parties and on the "costs" of entry (and exit) for minor parties. If the number of primaries is dramatically reduced, there might be no need to provide public funding to individual candidates. After the nominations, parties should be permitted to give money to their candidates above and beyond the existing public funding. New parties not receiving public funding should not be subject to contribution ceilings.

Among political scientists today, one finds a growing belief that the American party system has lost its capacity to set the political agenda and to initiate and sustain major political changes.[15] Although

[15] See, for example, Samuel Beer, "Federalism, Nationalism and Democracy in America," *American Political Science Review* (March 1978), p. 17; and Walter Dean Burnham, "Revitalization and Decay: Looking toward the Third Century of American Electoral Politics," *Journal of Politics*, vol. 38 (August 1976), pp. 146-73.

I have argued that the party system's role in this respect has not been as great as many have supposed—and not nearly as great as party-government advocates would like—parties did provide, nevertheless, one important means in the past by which to effect major shifts in the direction of public policy. During periods of realignment, the party system helped to redefine the scope and sometimes even the ends of government activity. It performed this function not with a radical bias in favor of innovation, but, if anything, with a conservative presumption against it. The decline of the party system's role as a regulator of political change and the partial assumption of this function by individual aspirants and the media have begun to alter the regime's basic posture toward change, albeit in ways that are not yet entirely clear. Although the new electoral process for the selection of the president was established in order to make the system much more open to change, it has thus far managed only to raise expectations for fundamental new departures without supplying the political support to accomplish them. Perhaps its ultimate effect will be to remove any systematic bias toward change, leaving the results to be determined by the seemingly random factors that dominate the presidential selection process. Before the new system becomes firmly established, political leaders should reassess the effects of the recent party reforms and ask whether it is still possible to take meaningful steps to restore important functions to our party system.

7

Democratizing the Democratic Party

Donald M. Fraser

This essay describes the general course of political party reform over the last decade, assesses its impact on the functioning of the political parties, and proposes some further steps. The term "political party" refers both to the organized party and to the party voter. Most of the references in this essay are to the organized party—the voluntary association of political activists who make up our national, state, and local parties, who operate under rules of their own choosing, and who generally exist independently of any statutory scheme. The "party voter" refers to the larger group who usually favor the candidates of one party with their vote in primary and general elections but do little more. In general, it is the objective of the organized party to gain and hold the allegiance of the party voters and to swell their ranks. The interaction between the organized party and the party voter seeking a larger role in the organized party provides the milieu in which most of the party reform efforts have occurred.

The reforms have proceeded along two lines. One has resulted in new standards by which the state parties must select their delegates to the national nominating conventions. The other has aimed at improving the internal organization of the party.

Until recently, both major U.S. parties were loosely organized at the national level, with the national parties often characterized as confederations of state parties. The principal responsibilities of the national parties were to convene the presidential nominating conventions every four years and to serve as a link between the state parties and the president. From time to time the national parties have emerged from their passive role and attempted to activate state parties and communicate with party voters directly, but such efforts have been neither consistent nor continuous.

Neither party had a national constitution defining its structure or responsibilities. A resolution enacted at each quadrennial convention reconfirmed the existence and responsibilities of the party's national committee for the next four years.

The civil rights movement forced the Democratic party to begin to assert authority over the states' procedures for selecting delegates. In 1964 a challenge to the seating of delegates on the grounds of racial discrimination impelled the Democratic National Committee to require states to certify that they did not practice discrimination in the selection of their delegates. The more far-reaching reforms, however, arose from the experience of the party with antiwar activists who sought to influence the deliberations of the Democratic convention in Chicago in August 1968.

The Origins of Contemporary Party Reform

In 1968 the candidacies of Eugene McCarthy and Robert Kennedy were vigorously supported by opponents of U.S. involvement in the Vietnam war. Hoping to change American policy in Southeast Asia, they succeeded in dissuading Lyndon Johnson from seeking reelection. As they continued working to deny Vice-President Hubert Humphrey the nomination, they encountered a variety of structural obstacles which frustrated their efforts to elect sympathetic delegates.

A hastily convened group calling itself the Commission on the Democratic Selection of Presidential Nominees worked for several weeks in August 1968 to document these obstacles. Headed by Governor Harold Hughes of Iowa, with a half-dozen others who also opposed the Vietnam war (though not necessarily Humphrey's candidacy), the group's report asserted that:

> About forty per cent of the states provide that all or some of their delegates shall be selected by state party officials.
> . . . The delegates to these state conventions are selected by local party officials rather than by open caucuses in which voters can participate. Local party officials were themselves elected some two years before.
> . . . Over 600 delegates to the 1968 Convention were selected by processes which have included no means of voter participation since 1966.
> . . . In other [states] imposition of the unit rule has silenced minority preferences.
> . . . In at least two counties in Oklahoma and one congressional district in Missouri, conventions were held in secret.[1]

[1] "The Democratic Choice," report of the Commission on the Democratic Selection of Presidential Nominees, Washington, D.C., 1968.

The report referred to "widespread cynicism about the capability of the parties, especially the Democratic Party, to accommodate the expectations of emergent social forces." It contained a number of recommendations to the 1968 national convention for changes in the nominating procedure.

This commission was not a formal instrument of the Democratic party, but its report encouraged interested delegates to offer resolutions at the 1968 convention requiring that future convention delegates be selected through a process in which all Democratic voters have a "meaningful and timely" and "full and timely" opportunity to participate. The convention, meeting in late August, adopted these resolutions.

In February 1969 the chairman of the Democratic National Committee appointed a commission, chaired initially by Senator George McGovern and usually called the McGovern-Fraser Commission, to implement the new resolutions. The commission's report asserted that during 1968 "in at least 20 states there were no (or inadequate) rules for the selection of convention delegates, leaving the entire process to the discretion of a handful of party leaders" and that "more than one-third of the convention delegates had, in effect, already been selected prior to 1968—before either the major issues or the presidential candidates were known."[2]

The commission went on to point out that practices such as the unit rule, favorite son candidacies, secret caucuses, closed slate making, and proxy voting all served to frustrate those who sought to take part in the nominating process. It also noted that there were excessive fees for participation in many cases and that the representation of blacks, women, and youth was well below their proportions in the population.

These allegations were well-grounded. Once these claims had been established, it was difficult for a Democrat to argue for the perpetuation of the old practices. The remedies, however, were to generate controversy.

The Reforms Enacted

The McGovern-Fraser Commission identified three kinds of practices that it argued violated the "full, meaningful and timely" language of the 1968 convention resolutions:

[2] "Mandate for Reform," report of the Commission on Party Structure and Delegate Selection to the Democratic National Committee, Washington, D.C., April 1970.

• Inhibiting access to the nominating process through excessive fees, excessively strict rules for registration, discrimination on the basis of race, national origin, age, or sex, or the unavailability of clearly written rules.

• Diluting the effect of participation through the use of proxy voting, quorum provisions, unit rules, apportionment, and so forth.

• Other problems such as inadequate public notice, automatic delegates, premature delegate selection, slate making, and so on.

The commission recommended specific rules to end each of these practices.

With respect to representation of blacks, women, and youth, the commission agreed that it could not impose quotas, but it did require state parties, first, to take affirmative action to encourage representation of these groups in the delegations to the national conventions and, second, to set as a goal for representation of these groups their proportion of the population of the state.

The commission, noting that full and meaningful participation is "precluded unless the presidential preference of each Democrat is fairly represented at all levels of the process," urged a proportional system of voting, but concluded that it lacked the power to require this of the state parties. It urged that the 1972 convention make such a rule binding.

The new delegate selection rules proposed by the commission were accepted by the Democratic National Committee later that year and made effective for the 1972 convention. That convention established the proportional voting system for delegate selection that took effect in 1976.

Republican Party Reform

At the outset the Democratic and Republican parties were organized in similar fashion. Neither party apportioned national convention delegates to the states strictly on the basis of party voters or population, and neither prescribed standards to guide states in choosing their delegates.

The Republicans have adopted some reforms since 1968. They forbid proxy voting, ban ex officio delegates, ban mandatory assessments for delegates, require that all caucus-convention proceedings be open, require the Republican National Committee to help state parties inform citizens about how they can participate in delegate selection procedures, and urge each state to have equal representation for men and women in its delegation. Apportionment for their national conventions remains as it was, however, despite a challenge from the Ripon Society. Affirmative action is not required, proportional voting is not required, and other detailed standards governing delegate selection are largely absent.

A paper by Charles Longley gives an interesting account of the Republican reform efforts and spells out a number of reasons why the Republicans have not moved further along this road.[3] He asserts that no significant element within the GOP has been lobbying for party reform. He points to "political" barriers which include the existing apportionment formulas favoring the smaller states in both the national convention and the Republican National Committee, the view of many Republican National Committee members that the national party is merely an association of state parties, and the success of Richard Nixon at the polls in both 1968 and 1972, which enabled the White House to dictate the national party's organizational agenda. He then identifies "structural" barriers consisting of a four-stage gauntlet which reform had to run, beginning with the Republican National Committee's Rules Committee, the full Republican National Committee, the Rules Committee of the convention, and the full convention. Three of these stages Longley describes as "structurally biased to advantage those areas traditionally wary of tinkering with the rules of the game."

Appraising the Altered Nominating System

Have the reforms been successful? This question is hard to answer even if we knew by what standards success should be judged. For example, some would argue that success at the polls is the only yardstick to use in measuring the impact of the reforms. Others would assess the reforms in terms of their effect on the organized party and its ability to carry out its full range of functions: developing positions on public policy and electing other federal, state, and local candidates. The ultimate question might be, Is the nominating process improving the ability of our nation to govern itself wisely and successfully—with all that implies?

These are not easily answered questions. Some argue that electing a candidate no matter what he or she stands for is not necessarily best—a political party must stand for a cluster of ideas and ideals, and

[3] "Party Reform and the Republican Party," prepared for delivery at the meeting of the American Political Science Association, New York City, 1978.

to abandon these in pursuit of power does not always serve the public interest. Others assert that no matter what the eventual consequences, it is indefensible to operate a nominating system that is patently unfair or discriminatory toward the party voter who wishes to participate.

The difficulty in demonstrating the consequences of the reforms is that almost any proposition about their effect can be supported or questioned by citing cases in point. The reforms were blamed for the nomination and defeat of McGovern in 1972, but the unreformed Republicans in 1964 had a comparable experience with Barry Goldwater. Jimmy Carter, who was nominated and elected after the reforms, may not be able to offer strong, effective leadership, but John Kennedy was almost completely frustrated in seeking enactment of his legislative programs before he died in 1963.

One of the difficulties in making an evaluation lies in the turbulence of events since the early 1960s, including assassinations, the civil rights revolution, the Vietnam war, Watergate, the energy crisis, and the new women's and environmental movements. The Vietnam war continued to play a major role after 1968. It energized a whole generation of Americans and deeply polarized the Democratic constituencies. As the party moved into the 1972 nominating season, this polarization played a major role in the dynamics of the nominating process. The 1972 election was followed by the Watergate scandal, which not only drove a president from office for the first time in our history, but left in its wake unprecedented cynicism and disillusionment with government. It would be expecting too much of any nominating system to hope that candidates could sail upon tranquil waters with such stormy seas about. To suppose that any nominating system, no matter what kind, could be insulated from the turbulence produced by these events is not only unthinkable, but in a democracy, undesirable.

As one ponders the issue, the suspicion grows that the mechanics of the nominating system may have far less to do with the kind of nominee selected than do such factors as the general climate of public opinion, the degree of political cohesion, the issues troubling the public, the qualities and records of the contending candidates, public attitudes toward the record and performance of the parties, and so on. Carter's successful nomination bid in 1976 illustrates the point. He was the only candidate who seemed to bridge the gaps between party factions polarized by the Vietnam war and the longer-standing North-South divisions within the party. Other candidates had track records that tied them to one of the factions.

Specific Criticisms of the Reforms

Certain changes by the Democrats following 1968 have drawn persistent criticism and need to be examined more closely. These include:

- the "quota" issue which arose in relation to the representation of women, minorities, and youth
- the use of proportional voting systems
- the proliferation of presidential primaries
- the diminished role of party leaders in negotiating the choice of a nominee.

The "Quota" in Delegate Selection. The "quota" issue probably has little impact upon the outcome of a contest for a party nomination. The issue arose after state parties were notified prior to the 1972 convention that the burden of proof would fall upon them to show that they had carried out the requisite affirmative action programs if they arrived at the convention with unbalanced delegations. Many state parties took the path of least resistance. They sought a balanced delegation in the reasonable expectation that this would avoid a challenge.

The Democrats have continued to wrestle with this problem and have taken steps to modify the procedures. Nonetheless, state delegations will continue to be under pressure to take affirmative steps to encourage greater participation by underrepresented groups. The question of women's participation is now settled by requiring an equal division of men and women in the national delegations. The only impact that the "quota" issue may have had on the nominating process was the possible displacement of a veteran party worker in favor of a representative of an underrepresented group. The trade-off for the organized party has been greater legitimacy for the process in the eyes of those belonging to the underrepresented groups, while risking the displeasure of the traditional party workers.

Proportional Voting. The use of proportional systems of voting is drawing mixed reviews. Some claim that it not only provides a means to assure that every point of view is fairly reflected at each stage of the process, but that it has the practical value of easing intraparty tension. When party voters attend a caucus or convention, they leave with the good feeling that they were treated fairly, without the polarizing effects of "winner-take-all" majority voting.

On the other hand, with the increase in single-issue politics, especially around the abortion issue, it is argued that proportional voting has the effect in caucus states of creating parties within parties. Those who feel strongly about one issue converge and send their most militant representatives upward through the process. These representatives owe their election only to their own group. There is no need, under this process, to produce delegates with broad appeal or to engage in the coalition building that majority voting often requires.

The current intrusion of single-issue politics is, of course, only another manifestation of the same phenomenon as when the issue was the Vietnam war.

A number of state parties are finding that under the new rules presidential politics dominates many other party decisions such as choosing state and local party officers and candidates. Proportional voting, linked with the requirement that at every stage of the process those seeking to be delegates must state their presidential preference, has the effect of defining the various factional groupings and their relative strengths in making other party decisions, often to the distress of state party leaders. This appears to be one reason why some state parties opted for presidential primaries. It insulates their state party from the politics of the presidential nomination.

It is probably too early to make an assessment of the trade-offs involved in the use of proportional voting. From the party voter's point of view, the proportional system seems fairer. The long-range effect upon the organized party system, however, will not be discernible until we have passed through several more seasons of presidential politics.

In the presidential primary states, certainly, proportional voting prevents the accidents of various combinations of candidates from awarding all the delegates to a candidate who may obtain a plurality of the votes but falls short of a majority. In the meantime, its impact upon the outcome of the nominating process itself, measured by the kind of nominee produced at the national convention, remains conjectural.

Proliferation of Presidential Primaries. The increased use of presidential primaries has drawn a great deal of criticism. This was one change the reformers did not intend, although the rhetoric of many of the reformers at first identified the presidential primary as a means of assuring greater participation without the arbitrary constraints imposed by state party leaders.

The problem is twofold. Primaries work to the disadvantage of the organized party by diminishing its role in the selection of a presidential nominee. Even more serious is their potential impact on the quality of the decision making in selecting a presidential nominee.

On the first point, of course, some state party leaders saw an advantage in insulating presidential politics from their state party processes. But because presidential politics attracts by far the greatest interest from party voters, the exclusion of presidential issues from the organized party means that the party is far less likely to benefit from the interest and participation of the party voter. This means missed opportunities for the organized party to build a broader base of workers and financial supporters, as well as to create a larger pool of active party members from which to choose in selecting candidates for party or public office.

The reasons for the dramatic growth in presidential primaries over the last decade are varied. When the McGovern-Fraser Commission began its work in 1969, seventeen states had presidential primaries. Few on the commission favored their expanded use. There was, however, no consensus about the need for an outright ban on primaries, because many saw some value in having a limited number of them. All agreed that the convention resolutions provided no basis for a rule favoring either presidential primaries or caucus-convention systems.

By 1972 the number of states with presidential primaries had grown to twenty-three, and by 1976, to thirty-one. By then 72 percent of the delegates to the Democratic national convention were being chosen by presidential primaries. This caused considerable alarm among many Democrats, and in 1975 a new party commission, chaired by Michigan Democratic Chairman Morley Winograd, was established by the Democratic party chairman to look into the growing number and ramifications of presidential primaries.

In explaining the expanded use of presidential primaries, the Winograd Commission reported that there are "two explanations for periodic public pressure to increase the use of presidential primaries. The first is political; people have justified the institution of primaries by arguing that parties as organizations are undemocratic and that primaries are more representative of the popular will." [4] The report goes on to note:

> One can interpret the proliferation of primaries following 1968 as a response to the McGovern-Fraser reforms. Dele-

[4] "Openness, Participation and Party Building: Reforms for a Stronger Democratic Party," report of the Commission on Presidential Nomination and Party Structure, Washington, D.C., February 1978.

> gate selection processes in 1968 were criticized as closed to rank and file participation. The reformers emphasized the value of participation in the delegate selection process. While the McGovern-Fraser Commission was officially neutral on the question of primaries, many state parties felt that because primaries increased rank and file participation in delegate selection adoption of a primary would open up the process. Since the new rules for delegate selection were evolving, many states also felt that a primary offered the most protection against a challenge at the next convention.
>
> When asked by the Commission staff, all but one of the state chairs whose state adopted a primary in the 1968–76 period said that the primary strengthened their state parties by allowing more Democrats to participate in the process.
>
> Another explanation of the move to primaries is that states wished to separate state politics from national politics. In the late sixties the national party was seriously divided over the Vietnam war. Involvement by state parties in national politics had the potential to seriously divide state parties as well.
>
> Prior to 1976 some states adopted primaries because they wanted the media attention provided when presidential candidates converge for a primary. Some states adopted primaries to try to become part of unofficial regional primaries. Two state chairs said that their states adopted a primary because George McGovern's supporters had taken over their caucuses in 1972.

One fact is indisputable: the experiences of 1968 and 1972 in the Democratic party focused interest on the nominating process. Arguably, if the party reforms designed to remove the obstacles and inequities facing those who sought to participate in the presidential nomination in 1968 had been in place prior to that time, there would have been far less criticism of the nominating process and thus less of a movement toward state presidential primaries.

The increased use of presidential primaries makes campaigning for the presidential nomination more expensive, tends to give advantages to candidates who are better known at the beginning of the nominating season, yields to the media a far larger role in influencing the outcome, and lessens the prospects for achieving the political cohesion needed among the elected officials of that party to govern successfully. It diminishes the role of the party leadership in helping to choose the candidates who will be best able to govern, a point made about the reform rules themselves.

The Reduced Role of Party Leaders. There can be little doubt about the impact of the Democratic party reforms on the role of the party leaders. Perhaps the extreme case makes the point. In Georgia, before the reforms, the delegates to the national convention were selected by the state party chair with the advice and consent of the governor, with the state party chair effectively being chosen by the governor.

In most of the other states, the practices were not so far out of line with the new rules, but under these rules governors, senators, state party chairs, and other potential brokers no longer had the influence or control over state delegations that they had wielded in the past. It can be argued with considerable force that this represents a real loss in the parties' ability to synthesize all the varied considerations that should go into the picking of a presidential nominee. The existence of these power brokers across the nation might be compared to the original notion behind the electoral college, when it was believed that a collegium of persons of sound judgment would produce the best president for the United States. This view seems to lie behind the lament often heard from the AFL-CIO that the old system which picked Franklin Roosevelt, Truman, and Kennedy was good enough for them.

The problem here is that once the legitimacy of the old ways was challenged, the national party had little choice but to acquiesce in a movement toward procedures that were more defensible under the values of a democratic society. The reforms could not promise wiser choices, certainly, but they could improve the climate of openness and fairness associated with the nominating process.

The Challenge Ahead

The real challenge to the parties, then, is how to proceed in light of the changed expectations of those who want a role in the nominating process. This challenge is heightened by the apparent decline in the party system itself.

A rising tide of public comment asserts that our party system is in trouble. The party voter's allegiance to the party-labeled candidate is weakening. Turnout at the polls is dropping. There is a proliferation of single-issue organizations. Finally, the voters appear increasingly alienated from our political and governmental system.

Some of these trends began before 1968, particularly the weakening of party loyalties and the decline in the turnout of voters at the polls. The increase in single-issue politics is more recent, and the general alienation of the voters has increased dramatically during the

1970s. The emergence of television as a principal means of reaching the voter has made its own contribution to this disarray.

The problems seem to be worsening. A triangular relationship seems to have developed among the political parties, the voters, and public officials, with the interactions generating a downward spiral of confidence and political cohesion. The perceptions of the voters as they view the performance of public officials reinforces their negative views, which in turn further weakens political cohesion and the capacity to act effectively.

A good illustration of this process is in our energy policies. A widely shared view is that a reduction in dependence upon foreign sources of energy will only come with conservation brought on by higher prices. The U.S. government can easily raise prices through excise taxes, and it can do so without hurting middle and lower income groups by providing them refundable tax credits. Yet President Carter's proposal for a yearly increase of five cents over the next ten years was never introduced into Congress because it had so little support. The reason it had so little support was not because of organized opposition, but because members of Congress believed it would be unpopular with the voters. Giving soft answers to hard problems reinforces the negative public attitudes toward our political and governmental institutions.

A nation whose political institutions provide these soft responses may be in ever deeper trouble as it heads into the next century. During the coming years we will face increased competition for diminishing supplies of energy and raw materials. This competition will become increasingly intense as world population grows and as development continues to raise consumption levels in the poorer two-thirds of the world.

One thoughtful writer, Robert Heilbroner, takes an even more apocalyptic view of the future of the Western democracies. He believes they will be unable to cope with this rising level of stress and will be forced to adopt more authoritarian regimes.[5]

The Plight of the Majority Party

The Democratic party today faces its own special difficulties. If one believes that our major parties are grounded in the economic self-interest of their adherents, one searches in vain for the economic issues that will reunite the Democrats. The cohesion that developed during the depths of the Great Depression is wearing away. The

[5] *An Inquiry into the Human Prospect* (New York: W. W. Norton, 1977).

principal economic issue over the last decade has been inflation, hardly an issue to unite the Democrats. In fact, it is almost a runaway issue in the other direction, leading to Proposition 13 and the moves toward a constitutional amendment for a balanced budget. The social issues of the last decade have further divided the traditional constituencies of the Democratic party, as Everett Carll Ladd, Jr., has effectively demonstrated in his recent book.[6]

Henry Fairlie sums up the plight of the Democrats in harsh terms:

> The Democratic party is almost dramatically holding its own as the normal majority party of the country after almost half a century. But as a governing party it is sadly uncertain of what it wants to do. What has been most clearly missing —in 1968 and in 1972, and again in 1976—is any forcible conception in the Democratic party itself of what it would like a Democratic president to accomplish. . . . The Democratic party at the moment is without a public philosophy; and a governing party without such a philosophy is a danger both to the country it governs and to itself.[7]

Where We Go from Here

Our objectives must be to recreate a public philosophy for the majority party, restore political cohesion to our parties, reawaken voter interest, and end voter cynicism. Can this be done by altering the workings of our organized parties?

This seems like a tall order. Yet in viewing the choices before us, the organized party may offer one of the few opportunities we have to influence the ways in which our political and governmental system will respond to future public problems.

The Role of the Organized Party. Probably the most elementary role of the organized party is to set the rules for the competition among those who seek political power or public office. In this view, the party is a passive container into which are poured a mix of contenders with assorted philosophical or ideological baggage. The party per se is not a creative force—not an actor on the political stage. It merely provides the stage.

Most organized parties are, however, more complex than this description suggests. They elicit varying degrees of loyalty from large

---

[6] *Where Have All the Voters Gone?* (New York: W. W. Norton, 1977).

[7] *The Parties: Republicans and Democrats in This Century* (New York: St. Martin's Press, 1978).

numbers of active participants who identify the party with a set of general beliefs compatible with their own. Among themselves they develop hierarchies of formal and informal leaders and followers, often through interaction with public officeholders with whom they identify. One of the challenges for the organized parties is to harness this potential in steadily improving their own performance. This includes defining public policy choices, recruiting new adherents, carrying on political education, sponsoring or encouraging candidates for public office, and helping to elect candidates.

From the perspective of the general party voter and the public, the candidate or the officeholder is the most visible, tangible presence of a political party. They obtain the media coverage. Their views on public policy help to shape party philosophy. Their performance in office adds to or detracts from the public image of the party itself.

Moreover, from the point of view of the party activist (the member of the organized party), electing candidates who perform their offices effectively within the framework of the party's philosophy represents the achievement of what the struggle in politics is all about. While a few political parties may be content with advancing ideas or ideologies, the major parties regard the achievement of public office as the ultimate justification for all their labors.

The Importance of the Party in Candidate Selection. Thus, the selection of candidates for office represents the single most important function the organized party can perform. The members of the organized party generally know the candidates best; they are familiar with their personal qualities of thoughtfulness, integrity, concern, and understanding. They are in the best position to take into account a myriad of considerations affecting electability and performance and to make recommendations to the party voter accordingly. To deny the party voter and ultimately the total electorate the benefit of this knowledge is a disservice to the community. Only through the organized party can a deliberate effort be made to improve upon the selection of candidates and at the same time to recreate the political cohesion among public officeholders of the same party that is necessary for effective governing.

To the extent that the organized party abdicates responsibility for the selection of its candidates, it becomes almost irrelevant to the solution of the problems facing our nation. Candidates and their supporters struggle to achieve the party nomination, but they are on their own insofar as the organized party is concerned, at least until after they have achieved the party's nomination.

In some respects, the organized parties in many states have already abdicated responsibility. The imposition of state party primaries in the early years of this century certainly made the role of the organized party more difficult, though not impossible, in promoting candidates for office. Those organized parties that could win and hold the respect of their party voter have been free to make recommendations to that party voter about the candidates they believe will best serve the interests of the community, state, or nation. Thus, some state parties have continued the practice of preprimary endorsements and have been able to prevail in state primary systems. Under these circumstances, the primary can be seen as a useful check on state parties that become corrupt, lazy, or indifferent to the concerns of the party voters. For most state parties, however, the challenge of the primary has been too severe, leading them to abandon preprimary endorsement for most if not all offices. The parties thus disable themselves from informing the party voter of their views concerning the respective merits of the candidates. The antiparty mood in some states has, of course, made party endorsements a liability to a candidate—or so it often seems in a state like New York.

Selecting a Presidential Nominee. The selection of a presidential nominee is by far the most important decision a political party makes. The nomination and subsequent election of the right kind of leadership to the presidency is the single most potent remedy available to reverse the disintegration of our political processes.

Where state legislatures have imposed state presidential primaries, the organized party loses any role. If the organized party is not constrained by a state presidential primary, however, it is free to develop and present its view on the merits of the various candidates for the presidential nomination as it proceeds with the election of delegates through a caucus-convention system or some variation thereof. In this process it is a legitimate role for the party leader or officeholder to influence the members of the organized party in their presidential preferences, a role that need not be diminished by the new rules although the leader may have to make a much greater effort to achieve the desired influence.

The national party could assist the organized state parties in achieving or retaining an active role in the selection of delegates to the national convention. It could establish further guidelines restricting somewhat the use of presidential primaries. It could facilitate opportunities for the members of the organized party to learn more about the potential candidates for the presidential nomination. This can be done in many ways, including more extensive communications with the organized party members about the potential candidates. The national party could sponsor meetings at the national, regional, or state level at which these party members could meet and talk with prospective nominees and listen to their platform presentation while avoiding the appearance of making an early commitment to a particular candidate. Such an effort was made in 1975 within the Democratic party by an informal coalition known as the Democratic Conference. The conference sponsored a series of five regional forums to which party activists were invited to hear the presidential candidates. President Carter came to several of them. The Republican party in 1979 was sponsoring these kinds of meetings for prospective presidential candidates.

Strengthened National Parties Needed. To carry on these kinds of programs successfully, however, the national party itself must take on a stronger institutional presence that gives it more resources and a greater capacity to act. A strengthened role for the national party is not easily achieved. Chronically underfinanced (as at least the Democratic party is), it finds that as soon as it gains control of the White House its role becomes totally subordinated to the wishes of the incumbent president. Presidents who have little sense of party or who feel no responsibility to help strengthen the party for the long term have been the rule, not the exception.

An interesting case in point is the Winograd Commission. It was begun in 1975 to review the issues raised by the proliferation of presidential primaries, but upon the election of President Carter it found its membership expanded and its interest deflected into proposals apparently aimed at making a challenge to the incumbent more difficult. This is in part the fault of the national party itself, which has not established a tradition of serving the broader interest of the party rather than simply the interest of an incumbent. Often, of course, the two interests converge. But recalling the lack of accountability of Nixon to any party body, there is both a public as well as a party interest in maintaining a modicum of independence from absolute control by the White House.

A number of proposals to strengthen the role of the national Democratic party have been made, and they deserve further consideration:

- Rework the present regional structure which divides the state Democratic parties into four regions. These regions are too large to be effective. We should have many more smaller regions. Regional activity by the national party is important and should be increased.

- Enhance the ability of the national office to provide research staff to party committees concerned with various sectors of public policy.
- Create a strong program of political education for all levels of the party, encouraging state parties to develop similar programs. Their content would range from a study of the history of the Democratic party, through techniques for organizing and campaigning, to a study of contemporary issues.
- Establish a national party membership in order to assist the national party in raising adequate funds. Limit participation in the selection of delegates to the midterm conferences to those members, but provide that no one be excluded for lack of ability to pay a membership fee.
- Enhance the planning and participation for midterm conferences and extend their length. Consider building each conference around one or two major issues.
- Improve the ability of the national party to publish reports, newsletters, and other material to maintain communication with party members.
- Establish a staff position to develop and maintain contact with political parties and movements in other nations, and encourage U.S. party activists to participate in meetings abroad as feasible.

In general, it is important in building a stronger national party to increase the numbers of state party activists who have an opportunity to take part in activities across state lines. This will enlarge the pool of party adherents who can contribute a national perspective to party decisions, including the most important one of all, the selection of a nominee for the presidency of the United States.

APPENDIX

In Defense of the American Party System

Edward C. Banfield

This essay, written at the beginning of the 1960s, is appended for the help it provides in thinking about the underlying causes of the changes that have occurred in American political parties in the intervening twenty years, and for the grave question it raises about the future of democratic politics.

The American party system has been criticized on four main grounds: (1) The parties do not offer the electorate a choice in terms of fundamental principles; their platforms are very similar and mean next to nothing; (2) they cannot discipline those whom they elect, and therefore they cannot carry their platforms into effect; (3) they are held together and motivated less by political principle than by desire for personal, often material, gain, and by sectional and ethnic loyalties; consequently party politics is personal and parochial; and (4) their structure is such that they cannot correctly represent the opinion of the electorate; in much of the country there is in effect only one party, and everywhere large contributors and special interests exercise undue influence within the party.[1]

NOTE: Reprinted from *Political Parties, U.S.A.*, ed. Robert A. Goldwin (Chicago: Rand McNally, 1961). Used by permission of the Public Affairs Conference Center, Kenyon College, Gambier, Ohio.

[1] These criticisms are made, for example, by the French political scientist, Maurice Duverger, in *Political Parties* (New York: Wiley, 1954). For similar criticisms by Americans, see especially Committee on Political Parties of the American Political Science Association, *Toward a More Responsible Two-Party System* (New York: Rinehart, 1950), and E. E. Schattschneider, *Party Government* (New York: Farrar & Rinehart, 1942). Criticisms of American parties are summarized and analyzed in Austin Ranney, *The Doctrine of Responsible Party Government* (Urbana: University of Illinois Press, 1954). Defenses of the American party system include A. Lawrence Lowell, *Essays on Government* (Boston: Houghton Mifflin, 1889), Chs. I, II; Arthur N. Holcombe, *The Political Parties of Today* (New York: Harper,

These criticisms may be summarized by saying that the structure and operation of the parties do not accord with the theory of democracy or, more precisely, with that theory of it which says that everyone should have a vote, that every vote should be given exactly the same weight, and that the majority should rule.

"It is a serious matter," says Maurice Duverger, a French political scientist who considers American party organization "archaic" and "undemocratic," "that the greatest nation in the world, which is assuming responsibilities on a world-wide scale, should be based on a party system entirely directed towards very narrow local horizons."[2] He and other critics of the American party system do not, however, base their criticisms on the performance of the American government. They are concerned about procedures, not results. They ask whether the structure and operation of the parties is consistent with the logic of democracy, not whether the party system produces—and maintains—a good society, meaning, among other things, one in which desirable human types flourish, the rights of individuals are respected, and matters affecting the common good are decided, as nearly as possible, by reasonable discussion.[3]

If they were to evaluate the party system on the basis of results, they would have to conclude that on the whole it is a good one. It has played an important part (no one can say how important, of course, for innumerable causal forces have been at work along with it) in the production of a society which, despite all its faults, is as near to being a good one as any and nearer by far than most; it has provided governments which, by the standards appropriate to apply to governments, have been humane and, in some crises, bold and enterprising; it has done relatively little to impede economic growth and in some ways has facilitated it; except for the Civil War, when it was, as Henry Jones Ford said, "the last bond of union to give way,"[4] it has tended to check violence, moderate conflict, and narrow the cleavages within the society; it has never produced, or very seriously threatened to produce, either mob rule or tyranny, and it has shown a marvelous ability to adapt to changing circumstances.

1925); and *Our More Perfect Union* (Cambridge: Harvard University Press, 1950); Pendleton Herring, *The Politics of Democracy* (New York: Norton, 1940); and Herbert Agar, *The Price of Union* (Boston: Houghton Mifflin, 1950).

[2] *Op. cit.*, p. 53.

[3] The report of the Committee on Parties of the American Political Science Association, cited above, discusses the "effectiveness" of parties entirely in terms of procedure. Duverger does the same.

[4] Henry Jones Ford, *The Rise and Growth of American Politics* (New York: Macmillan, 1900), p. 303.

Not only has the American party system produced good results, it has produced better ones than have been produced almost anywhere else by other systems. Anyone who reflects on recent history must be struck by the following paradox: those party systems that have been most democratic in structure and procedure have proved least able to maintain democracy; those that have been most undemocratic in structure and procedure—conspicuously those of the United States and Britain—have proved to be the bulwarks of democracy and of civilization.

This paper explores this paradox. It maintains that there is an inherent antagonism between "democracy of procedure" and "production of, and maintenance of, a good society"; that some defects of procedure are indispensable conditions of success from the standpoint of results, and that what the critics call the "archaic" character of the American party system is a very small price to pay for government that can be relied upon to balance satisfactorily the several conflicting ends that must be served.

Difficulties in Planning Change

Before entering into these matters, it may be well to remind the reader how difficult is the problem of planning social change.

Social relationships constitute systems: they are mutually related in such a manner that a change in one tends to produce changes in all of the others. If we change the party system in one respect, even a seemingly trivial one, we are likely to set in motion a succession of changes which will not come to an end until the whole system has been changed. The party system, moreover, is an element of a larger political system and of a social system. A small change in the structure or operation of parties may have important consequences for, say, the family, religion, or the business firm.

The changes that we intend when making a reform, if they occur at all, are always accompanied by others that we do not intend. These others may occur at points in the system far removed from the one where the change was initiated and be apparently unrelated to it. Commonly changes produced indirectly and unintentionally turn out to be much more important than the ones that were sought. This is a fact that is seldom fully taken into account. Those who support a particular reform are often indifferent to its consequences for values that they either do not share or consider subordinate. Even those who feel obliged to take a wide range of values into account do not usually try very hard to anticipate the indirect consequences of reforms—

often for a very good reason: the complexity of the social system makes the attempt implausible. Usually we take it on faith that the consequences we get by intention justify the risk we take of incurring others that we do not intend or want. Since these others are seldom recognized as consequences of our action at all (they either go unnoticed or seem to have "just happened"), the basis of our faith is not called into question.

No doubt it is a great help to the practical reformer to have tunnel vision. But those who are concerned with the welfare of society as a whole must take the widest perspective possible. They must try to identify all of the consequences that will follow from a reform—the unintended ones no less than the intended, the remote, contingent, and imponderable no less than the immediate, certain, the specifiable. And they must evaluate all of these consequences in the light of a comprehensive system of values.

Those who devise "improvements" to a social system can rarely hope to attain all of their ends; usually they must be prepared to sacrifice some of them to achieve others. This is so because resources are usually limited and also because there are often incompatibilities among ends such that a gain in terms of some necessarily involves a loss in terms of others. The reformer must therefore economize. He must be able to assign priorities to all ends in such a way that he can tell how much of each to sacrifice for how much of others, on various assumptions as to "supply."

The critics of the party system tend to value democratic procedure for its own sake, that is, apart from the results it produces. There is no reason why they should not do so. But they are in error when they do not recognize that other values of equal or greater importance are often in conflict with democratic procedure, and that when they are, some sacrifice of it is essential in order to serve the other values adequately. If they faced up to the necessity of assigning priorities among all of the relevant ends, they would not, it is safe to say, put "democratic procedure" first. Probably they, and most Americans, would order the ends as follows:

1. The party system must above all else provide governments having the will and capacity to preserve the society and to protect its members. Any sacrifice in other ends ought to be accepted if it is indispensable to securing this end.

2. The party system must insure periodic opportunity to change the government by free elections. Any sacrifice of other ends (except the one above) ought to be accepted if it is indispensable to securing this one.

3. The party system should promote the welfare of the people. By "welfare" is meant some combination of two kinds of values: "principles," what is thought to be good for the society, described in rather general terms, and "interests," the ends individuals and groups seek to attain for their own good, as distinguished from that of the society. The party system should produce governments that assert the supremacy of principles over interests in some matters; in others it should allow interests to prevail and should facilitate the competitive exercise of influence.

4. The party system should moderate and restrain such conflict as would threaten the good health of the society. Other conflict it should not discourage.

5. The party system should promote and exemplify democracy, meaning reasonable discussion of matters affecting the common good in which every voice is heard.

These ends have been listed in what most Americans would probably consider a descending order of importance. In devising a party system, we ought not to try to serve fully each higher end before serving the one below it at all. The first two ends are exceptions to this rule, however: each of them must be attained even if the others are not served at all. With respect to the remaining three, the problem is to achieve a proper balance—one such that no reallocation from one end to another would add to the sum of value.

Finally, we must realize that we can rarely make important social changes by intention. The most we can do is to make such minor changes as may be consistent with, and more or less implied by, the fixed features of the situation in which we are placed. Even to make minor changes in an institution like a political party requires influence of a kind and amount that no group of reformers is likely to have or to be able to acquire. It is idle to propose reforms that are merely desirable. There must also be some possibility of showing, if only in a rough and conjectural way, that they might be carried into effect.

With respect to the American party system, it seems obvious that the crucial features of the situation are all fixed. The size of our country, the class and cultural heterogeneity of our people, the number and variety of their interests, the constitutionally-given fragmentation of formal authority, the wide distribution of power which follows from it, the inveterate taste of Americans for participation in the day-to-day conduct of government when their interests are directly at stake—these are all unalterable features of the situation. Taken together, they mean that the party system can be reformed only within very narrow limits.

A Model Party System

Let us imagine a system free of the alleged defects of ours. In this model system, every citizen is motivated—highly so—by political principles, not subsidiary ones, but ones having to do with the very basis of the society. (In France and Italy, Duverger says approvingly, political warfare "is not concerned with subsidiary principles but with the very foundations of the state and the nature of the regime."[5]) The electoral system, moreover, is such as to give every side on every issue exactly the weight that its numbers in the population warrant; no group or interest is over- or under-represented. ("One's thoughts turn," Duverger says, "to the possibility of a truly scientific democracy, in which parliament would be made up of a true sample of the citizens reproducing on a reduced scale the exact composition of the nation, made up, that is, according to the very methods that are used as a basis for public opinion surveys like the Gallup polls."[6])

Assuming that the society is divided by the usual number of cleavages (e.g., haves versus have-nots, segregationists versus anti-segregationists, isolationists versus internationalists, etc.), the following would result:

1. There would be a great many parties, for no citizen would support a party with which he did not agree fully.

2. The parties would tend to be single-issue ones. If logically unrelated issues (for instance, segregation and isolationism) were linked together in a party program, only those voters would support the party who chanced to be on the same side of all of the linked issues. The number of these voters would decrease as the number of issues so linked increased.

3. Parties would be short-lived. They would come into and pass out of existence with the single issues they were organized to fight.

4. In their election campaigns and propaganda, parties would emphasize their single defining principles. This would tend to widen the cleavages along which the parties were formed.

5. Ideological issues, not practical problems, would constitute the substance of politics.[7]

6. The number of such issues pressing for settlement at any one time (but being incapable of settlement because of their ideo-

---

[5] *Op. cit.*, p. 419.

[6] *Ibid.*, p. 158.

[7] In France, according to Siegfried, "every argument becomes a matter of principle; the practical results are relegated to second place." André Siegfried, "Stable Instability in France," *Foreign Affairs*, XXXIV (April 1956), 395.

logical character) would always be more than the system could accommodate.[8]

7. Coalitions of parties would seldom form, and such as did form would be highly unstable. Party leaders would find compromise almost impossible because it would lead to loss of highly principled supporters.

8. Coalitions of parties being unstable, governments would also be unstable and therefore lacking in power and decision.

9. Those selected for positions of political leadership would tend to be ideologues skilled in party dialectics and symbolizing the party and its positions. Practical men, especially those with a talent for compromise and those symbolizing qualities common to the whole society, would be excluded from politics.

10. Matters having no ideological significance (a category that includes most local issues) would either be endowed with a spurious one or else would be left outside the sphere of politics altogether.[9]

These points should suffice to show that a system with a perfectly democratic structure would not produce results acceptable in terms of the criteria listed above.

Now let us introduce into the model system one of the alleged defects which the critics find most objectionable in the American party system. Let us suppose that at least half of the electorate is prevailed upon to exchange its vote in matters of fundamental principle for advantages that have nothing to do with principle, especially private profit, sectional gain, and nationality "recognition."

One effect of this would be to reduce greatly the intensity of ideological conflict and to make political life more stable and conservative. This, in fact, seems to be what happened when American parties first came into being. John Adams tells in his diary how in 1794 "ten thousand people in the streets of Philadelphia, day after day, threatened to drag Washington out of his house and effect a revolution in the government, or compel it to declare war in favor of the French Revolution and against England."[10] After parties had been

---

[8] According to Siegfried: "The difficulty is that too many questions of fundamental importance on which the various parties have cause to disagree have come up for decision at one time." *Ibid.*, p. 399.

[9] In France, Luethy says, "politics," which deals with ideological matters, and the "state," i.e., the bureaucracy, which deals with practical ones, function "in water-tight compartments" with the consequence that French democracy is an amalgam of absolutist administration on the one hand and of anarchy, tumultuous or latent, on the other. Herbert Luethy, *France Against Herself* (New York: Meridian Books, 1957), p. 61. On this see also Siegfried, *op. cit.*, p. 399.

[10] Quoted by Henry Jones Ford, *op. cit.*, p. 125.

organized, however, patronage took the place of ideological fervor. "The clubs of the social revolutionists which had sprung up in the cities, blazing with incendiary ideas caught from the French Revolution," Henry Jones Ford says, "were converted into party workers, and their behavior was moderated by considerations of party interest."[11]

Another effect would be to encourage the formation of a few (probably two) stable parties. These might begin as alliances among the profit-minded, the sectional-minded, and the nationality-minded, but to attract support from principled voters the parties would have to seem to stand for something—indeed, for anything and everything. Since no faction of them could hope to win an election by itself, principled voters would attach themselves to those parties that they found least objectionable. The parties would develop corporate identities and mystiques; principled voters would then subordinate their differences out of "loyalty" to the party and in response to its demands for "regularity." Competition for middle-of-the-road support would cause the parties to offer very similar programs. This competition might lead to there being only two parties, but this result would probably be insured by introducing another supposed defect into the system: a principle of representation (single-member districts and plurality voting) which, by letting the winner take all, would force small parties to join large ones in order to have some chance of winning.

In one way or another, the "defects" of the system would tend to produce these consequences—consequences which have in fact been produced in the United States:

1. A strong and stable government would be possible. The country would be governed by the party that won the election, or (given the particular complexities of the American system) by two closely similar parties engaged in give-and-take and, therefore, in a sense constituting one party under two names.

2. There would be a high degree of continuity between administrations elected from different parties. Elections would not shake the nation to its foundations because the competing parties would be fundamentally in agreement. Agreement would be so built in by countless compromises within the parties (each of which would be under the necessity of attracting middle-of-the-road support) that a change of party would seldom entail complete reversal of policy in an important matter.

---

[11] *Ibid.*, p. 144.

3. There would exist many substructures of power that would be largely or wholly impervious to the influence of political principle or ideology. "Machines"—party organizations of the profit-minded, the sectional-minded, and the nationality-minded—would not be inclined to offer pie in the sky or to stir the emotions of the masses because they could count upon getting their votes in other ways. These essentially apolitical centers of power would therefore exert a stabilizing and conservative influence throughout the political system. By making businesslike deals with the leaders of the "machines," the President could sometimes buy freedom to do as he thought best in matters of principle.

4. The diversity of the principles and the multiplicity of the interests within the party would be another source of strength to the leader elected from it. He could afford to offend some elements of the party on any particular question because there would be enough other elements unaffected (or even gratified) to assure his position. The more fragmented his party, the less attention he would have to pay to any one fragment of it.

5. The assertion of interests (as distinguished from principles) would be encouraged. The profit-minded, the sectional-minded, and the nationality-minded would in effect give up representation on matters of principle in order to get it on matters involving their interests. Thus two different systems of representation would work simultaneously. The party leader would act as a trustee, disregarding interests in favor of principles. ("Congress represents locality, the President represents the nation," Ford wrote in 1898.[12]) Meanwhile legislators dependent on machines and, in general, on profit-minded, sectional-minded, and nationality-minded voters would act as agents of interests. The trustee of principles (the President) and the agents of interests (Congressmen) would of necessity bargain with each other; by allowing the agents of interests some successes—but only in this way—the trustee of principles could win their support in the matters he considered most important. Thus, there would be achieved that balancing of interests and of interests against principles (the most important principles usually being vindicated) that a good party system should produce.

6. The formation of deep cleavages would nevertheless be discouraged. The competition of the parties for the middle-of-the-road vote; their tendency to select practical men of wide popular appeal,

[12] *Ibid.*, p. 187. For a recent brilliant account of how the two systems of representation work, see Willmoore Kendall, "The Two Majorities," *Midwest Journal of Political Science*, IV, No. 4 (November 1960), 317-345.

rather than ideologues, for positions of leadership; and the definition of the politicians' task as being that of finding the terms on which people who disagree will work together, rather than that of sharpening ideological points—these would all be unifying tendencies.

Some critics of the American party system have attributed its alleged defects to the absence of class consciousness in our society. No doubt there is some truth in this. But causality may run the other way also. We may be lacking in class consciousness because our politicians are prevented by the nature of the party system from popularizing the rhetoric of the class struggle; the party system actually induces the voter to forgo the allurements of principle and ideology by offering him things he values more: e.g., personal profit, sectional advantage, and nationality "recognition."[13]

In those countries where the voter expresses at the polls his ideology rather than his interests, he may do so not from choice but because the party system leaves him no alternative. In such countries, class warfare may be the principal subject-matter of politics simply because matters of greater importance to the voters are not at stake.

Experience in the underdeveloped areas seems to bear out the claim that certain "defects" in a party system may be essential to good government. The transplanted "defects" of the American party system are among the factors that have made the Philippines the most democratic country in Southeast Asia. According to Professor Lucian W. Pye:

> . . . the image of leadership that evolved in the Philippines was clearly that of the politican who looked after the particular interests of voters. Elsewhere the pattern of the Western impact under colonialism gave emphasis to the role of the rational administrator who apparently operated according to the principles of efficiency and who was not supposed to be influenced by political pressures within the society. Consequently, when the politicians emerged in these

[13] ". . . in coordinating the various elements of the populations for political purposes," Ford says, "party organization tends at the same time to fuse them into one mass of citizenship, pervaded by a common order of ideas and sentiments, and actuated by the same class of motives. This is probably the secret of the powerful solvent influence which American civilization exerts upon the enormous deposits of alien population thrown upon this country by the torrent of emigration. Racial and religious antipathies, which present the most threatening problems to countries governed upon parliamentary principles, melt with amazing rapidity in the warm flow of a party spirit which is constantly demanding, and is able to reward the subordination of local and particular interests to national purposes." (*Op. cit.*, pp. 306-307.)

> societies, they tended to become the champions of nationalistic ideologies and even the enemies of the rational administrators.[14]

In the Philippines, as at home, our party system has had the defects of its virtues—and the virtues of its defects. On the one hand, Pye says, the Philippines have never had an efficient administrative machinery, and the demand for higher standards of personal integrity among their public officials is reminiscent of the muckraking era of American politics; on the other hand, "the Philippine electorate seems to recognize that the most fundamental question in politics is who is going to control the government, and thus, while the parties have not had to expend much effort in trying to distinguish themselves ideologically from each other, the expenditures of money on political campaigns in the Philippines are probably the highest in proportion to per capita income of any country in the world."[15]

Making Parties "Responsible"

Some think that the American party system can be reformed without changing its nature essentially. Several years ago, a Committee on Parties of the American Political Science Association proposed making certain "readjustments" in the structure and operation of the party system to eliminate its "defects." These readjustments, the Committee said, would give the electorate "a proper range of choice between alternatives" in the form of programs to which the parties would be committed and which they would have sufficient internal cohesion to carry into effect. Thus, the two-party system would be made more "responsible."[16]

What this means is not at all clear. "Responsibility" here seems to be a synonym for accountability, that is, the condition of being subject to being called to account and made to take corrective action in response to criticism. In the case of a party, this can mean nothing except going before an electorate, and in this sense all parties are by definition responsible. "Responsibility" can have no other meaning in this context; as William Graham Sumner remarked, "a party is an abstraction; it cannot be held responsible or punished; if it is deprived of power it fades into thin air and the men who composed it, especially

---

[14] Lucian W. Pye, "The Politics of Southeast Asia," in G. Almond and J. Coleman (eds.), *The Politics of the Developing Areas* (Princeton, N.J.: Princeton University Press, 1960), p. 97. Copyright © 1960 by Princeton University Press.

[15] *Ibid.*, pp. 123 and 126.

[16] See the Committee Report, *op. cit.*, pp. 1 and 85.

those who did the mischief and needed discipline, quickly reappear in the new majority."[17]

Leaving aside both the question of what "responsibility" means when applied to a party and the more important one of whether as a matter of practical politics such "readjustments" could be made, let us consider how the political system would probably be affected by the changes proposed.

The hope that the two-party system might be made to offer a choice between distinct alternatives is illusory for at least two reasons. One is that a party which does not move to the middle of the road to compete for votes condemns itself to defeat and eventually, if it does not change its ways, to destruction. But even if this were not the case, the parties could not present the electorate with what reformers think of as "a valid choice." The reason is that the issues in our national life are such that there does not exist any one grand principle by which the electorate could be divided into two camps such that every voter in each camp would be on the "same" side of all issues. The idea of "left" and "right" is as close as we come to having such a grand principle, and it has little or no application to many issues.[18] The logic of "left" and "right" does not, for example, imply opposite or even different positions on (for example) foreign policy, civil liberties, or farm subsidies. Without a grand principle which will make unities—opposed unities—of the party programs, the electorate cannot be offered "a valid choice." A choice between two market baskets, each of which contains an assortment of unrelated items, some of which are liked and some of which are disliked, is not a "valid" choice in the same sense that a choice between two market baskets, each of which contains items that "belong together" is a "valid" one. In the American party system, most items are logically unrelated. This being so, "valid" choice would become possible only if the number of parties was increased to allow each party to stand for items that *were* logically related, if one issue became important to the exclusion of all the others, or if, by the elaboration of myth and ideology, pseudo-logical relations were established among items.

---

[17] William Graham Sumner, *The Challenge of Facts* (New Haven, Conn.: Yale University Press, 1914), pp. 271-272.

[18] One can imagine a set of symbols connected with a diffuse ideology dividing the society into two camps, and to a certain extent this exists. But it is hard to see in what sense this would present the electorate with "a valid choice." In other words, the existence of a body of nonsense which is treated as if it were a grand principle ought not to be regarded by reasonable critics of the party system as equivalent to the grand principle itself.

The hope that the parties might commit themselves to carry out their programs is also illusory. A party could do this only if its leaders were able to tell the President and the party members in Congress what to do, and could discipline them if they failed to do it. Therefore, unless, like the Russians, we were to have two sets of national leaders, one in governmental office and another much more important one in party office, it would be necessary for our elected leaders—in effect, the President, since only he and the Vice President are elected by the whole nation—to control the Congressmen and Senators of their party. This would be possible only if the President could deny re-election to members of Congress who did not support the party program. Thus, instead of merely bringing forward and electing candidates, as they do now, "responsible" parties would have to govern the country. We would have a parliamentary system with the President in a position somewhat like that of the British Prime Minister, except (a very important difference) that, not being a part of the legislature, he could not use it as a vehicle through which to exert his leadership.[19] The legislature would in fact have no function at all.

This great shift of power to the President would remedy another "defect" in the party system: its receptivity to the demands of interest groups.[20] With the President in full control of Congress, logrolling would cease or virtually cease. It would do so because no one could any longer make the President pay a price for assistance in getting legislation passed; the traders who now sell their bits and pieces of power to the highest bidders would have to lower their prices and would probably go out of business. With their opportunities for exercising influence vastly reduced, interest groups would be less enterprising both in their efforts to anticipate the effects of governmental action and in bringing their views to the attention of the policy makers.

The making of policy would thus pass largely into the hands of technical experts within the majority party, the White House, and the executive departments. These would be mindful of principles and

[19] The Prime Minister is the leader of his party outside as well as inside Parliament. Party leaders who are not also members of Parliament take no part in the running of the government, as the late Professor Harold Laski discovered when, as a leader of the Labour Party, he presumed to give advice to Prime Minister Attlee. The party leaders discipline their followers by threatening to deprive them of renomination; accordingly most members of the House are "backbenchers" who participate in its affairs only as audience, and the function of the House as a whole is to criticize and advise the leaders of the majority party.

[20] Cf. Report of the Committee on Parties, *op. cit.*, pp. 19-20.

impatient of interests. They would endeavor to make "coherent" policies, meaning, presumably, policies not based on compromise.[21] In all important matters, however, "the public interest" would prove an insufficient guide; the experts, when confronted with the necessity of choosing between alternatives that were equally in the public interest—that is, when no authoritative, ultimate criterion of choice existed for them to apply—would by the very necessities of the case have to balance the competing values as best they could, which means that they would have to fall back upon their personal tastes or professional biases.[22] Thus they would do badly (but in the name of "impartial administration") what is now done reasonably well by the political process.

The destruction of political traders and of local centers of power would mean also that the President's power would derive from somewhat different sources than at present. Instead of relying upon logrolling and patronage to get the votes he would need in Congress, he would have to rely upon direct appeals to the electorate. To some extent he might manipulate the electorate by charm and personality; TV and the arts of Madison Avenue would become more important in politics. But in order to get elected he would have to depend also, and to a greater extent, upon appeals to political principle or ideology. Whereas the political trader maintains his control by giving and withholding favors to individuals (a circumstance which makes his control both dependable in its operation and cheap), the President would have to maintain *his* by the uncertain and costly expedient of offering to whole classes of people—the farmer, the aged, the home owner, and so on—advantages that they would have only at each other's expense. If charm and the promise of "something for everybody" did not yield the amount of power he required to govern the country, the President might find it necessary to exploit whatever antagonisms within the society might be made to yield more power. Class and ethnic differences might in this event serve somewhat the same function as logrolling and patronage do now. Mayor LaGuardia, for example, depended for power upon direct, personal appeal to the voters rather than upon organization. His charm and his support of "liberal" programs are well remembered. But it should not be forgotten that he depended also upon exploitation of ethnic loyalties and antipathies. According to Robert Moses,

---

[21] *Ibid.*, p. 19.

[22] This argument is developed in E. C. Banfield, *Political Influence* (Glencoe, Ill.: Free Press, 1961), Ch. 12.

> It must be admitted that in exploiting racial and religious prejudices LaGuardia could run circles around the bosses he despised and derided. When it came to raking ashes of Old World hates, warming ancient grudges, waving the bloody shirt, tuning the ear to ancestral voices, he could easily out-demagogue the demagogues. And for what purpose? To redress old wrongs abroad? To combat foreign levy or malice domestic? To produce peace on the Danube, the Nile, the Jordan? Not on your tintype. Fiorello LaGuardia knew better. He knew that the aim of the rabble rousers is simply to shoo into office for entirely extraneous, illogical and even silly reasons the municipal officials who clean city streets, teach in schools, protect, house and keep healthy, strong and happy millions of people crowded together here.[23]

That a President might rely more upon appeals to political principle does not at all mean that better judgments or results would follow. For the discussion of principles would probably not be *serious;* it would be for the purpose of securing popular interest and consent, not of finding a wise or right course of action. As long ago as 1886, Sir Henry Sumner Maine observed that democracy was tending toward government by salesmanship. Party and corruption had in the past always been relied upon to bring men under civil discipline, he said, but now a third expedient had been discovered:

> This is generalization, the trick of rapidly framing, and confidently uttering, general propositions on political subjects. . . . General formulas, which can be seen on examination to have been arrived at by attending only to particulars few, trivial or irrelevant, are turned out in as much profusion as if they dropped from an intellectual machine; and debates in the House of Commons may be constantly read, which consisted wholly in the exchange of weak generalities and strong personalities. On a pure Democracy this class of general formulas has a prodigious effect. Crowds of men can be got to assent to general statements, clothed in striking language, but unverified and perhaps incapable of verification; and thus there is formed a sort of sham and pretence of concurrent opinion. There has been a loose acquiescence in a vague proposition, and then the People, whose voice is the voice of God, is assumed to have spoken.[24]

---

[23] Robert Moses, *LaGuardia: A Salute and a Memoir* (New York: Simon & Schuster, 1957), pp. 37-38. Copyright © 1957 by Simon & Schuster.

[24] Sir Henry Sumner Maine, *Popular Government* (New York: Henry Holt, 1886), pp. 106-108.

Efforts to create "levity of assent," as Maine called it, will become more important in our politics to the extent that other means of bringing men under civil discipline are given up or lost.

The Danger of Meddling

A political system is an accident. It is an accumulation of habits, customs, prejudices, and principles that have survived a long process of trial and error and of ceaseless response to changing circumstance. If the system works well on the whole, it is a lucky accident—the luckiest, indeed, that can befall a society, for all of the institutions of the society, and thus its entire character and that of the human types formed within it, depend ultimately upon the government and the political order.

To meddle with the structure and operation of a successful political system is therefore the greatest foolishness that men are capable of. Because the system is intricate beyond comprehension, the chance of improving it in the ways intended is slight, whereas the danger of disturbing its working and of setting off a succession of unwanted effects that will extend throughout the whole society is great.

Democracy must always meddle, however. An immanent logic impels it to self-reform, and if other forces do not prevent, it must sooner or later reform itself out of existence.[25]

The logic of this is as follows. The ideal of democracy legitimates only such power as arises out of reasonable discussion about the common good in which all participate. Power that comes into being in any other way (e.g., by corruption, logrolling, appeals to sentiment or prejudice, the exercise of charm or charisma, "hasty generalization," terror, etc.) is radically undemocratic, and people inspired by the democratic ideal will therefore endeavor to eliminate it by destroying, or reforming, whatever practices or institutions give rise to it.

No society, however, can be governed *solely* by reasonable discussion about the common good; even in a society of angels there might be disagreement about what the common good requires in the concrete case.[26] In most societies, far more power is needed to maintain civil discipline and protect the society from its enemies than can be got simply by reasonable discussion about the common good. Therefore the logical culmination of democratic reform, viz., the elimination of all undemocratic sources of power, would render

[25] For data and analysis pertinent to the discussion that follows, see James Q. Wilson, *The Amateur Democrat* (Chicago: University of Chicago Press, 1962).

[26] See Yves R. Simon, *The Philosophy of Democratic Government* (Chicago: University of Chicago Press, 1951), Ch. 1.

government—and therefore the preservation of the society—impossible. Democratic reform can never reach this point, of course, because, before reaching it, democracy itself would be destroyed and the impetus to further reform removed.

So far as it does succeed, however, the tendency of democratic reform is to reduce the power available for government. Such loss of power as occurs from the elimination of undemocratic sources of it will seldom be offset by increases in power of the kind that arises from reasonable discussion about the common good. Since there is a point beyond which no increase in democratic power is possible (the capacity of a society to engage in reasonable discussion about the common good being limited), reform, if carried far enough, must finally reduce the quantity of power.

There is, then, a danger that reform will chip away the foundations of power upon which the society rests. But this is not the only danger. A greater one, probably, is that in making some forms of undemocratic power less plentiful, reform may make others more plentiful, and by so doing set off changes that will ramify throughout the political system, changing its character completely. If, for example, politicians cannot get power by the methods of the machine (corruption, favor-giving, and patronage), they may get it by other methods, such as charm, salesmanship, and "hasty generalization." The new methods may be better than the old by most standards (they cannot, of course, be better by the standard of democracy, according to which *all* power not arising from reasonable discussion about the common good is absolutely illegitimate); but even if they are better, the new methods may not serve as well as the old, or may not serve at all, in maintaining an effective political system and a good society.

Reform is, of course, far from being the only force at work. Compared to the other forces, some of which tend to produce competing changes and others of which tend to check all change, reform may be of slight effect. This is certainly true in general of such reform as is sought through formal organizations by people called "reformers." It is much less true of reform in the broader sense of the general view and disposition of "the great body of right-thinking people." This kind of reform is likely to be of pervasive importance in the long run, although its effects are seldom what anyone intended.

Jefferson may have been right in saying that democracy cannot exist without a wide diffusion of knowledge throughout the society. But it may be right also to say that it cannot exist *with* it. For as we become a better and more democratic society, our very goodness and democracy may lead us to destroy goodness and democracy in the effort to increase and perfect them.

The Editor and the Authors

ROBERT A. GOLDWIN is a resident scholar and director of constitutional studies at the American Enterprise Institute. He served in the White House as special consultant to the president and, concurrently, as advisor to the secretary of defense. He taught at the University of Chicago and Kenyon College and was the dean of St. John's College in Annapolis. His edited books include *How Democratic Is America?*, *Left, Right and Center*, and *Political Parties, USA*.

EDWARD C. BANFIELD, George D. Markham Professor of Government at Harvard University, has written extensively on the politics and problems of American cities. His books include *City Politics*, with James Q. Wilson; *The Moral Basis of a Backward Society*, with Laura Banfield; and *The Unheavenly City*.

BENJAMIN R. BARBER is a professor of political science at Rutgers University, the editor of the journal *Political Theory*, and the author of *Superman and Common Men*, *The Death of Communal Liberty*, and (forthcoming) *The Strong Theory of Democracy*. He has written for *Harper's*, *The New Republic*, *Dissent*, and many scholarly journals, including *Daedalus*.

KENNETH A. BODE is a political correspondent for the National Broadcasting Company. He has been politics editor of *The New Republic* and a commentator on WNET-TV in New York City. He was research director of the Democratic party's Commission on Party Structure and Delegate Selection (the McGovern-Fraser Commission) and a member of the Mikulski and Winograd Commissions on party reform.

CAROL F. CASEY was a staff assistant for the Democratic party's Commission on Party Structure and Delegate Selection (the McGovern-Fraser Commission) and was the research director of the Mikulski Commission. She has also been head of the Political Institutions and Process Section in the Government Division of the Congressional Research Service and has worked for the 1980 Kennedy for President campaign.

JAMES W. CEASER is an assistant professor of government and foreign affairs at the University of Virginia. He is the author of *Presidential Selection* and coauthor of *Proportional Representation in the Presidential Nominating Process.*

DONALD M. FRASER was elected mayor of Minneapolis in 1979. He served as a member of the U.S. House of Representatives from 1963 to 1978, representing Minnesota's fifth congressional district. He was chairman (after Senator McGovern) of the Democratic party's Commission on Party Structure and Delegate Selection, 1971–1972; member of the Commission on the Role and Future of Presidential Primaries, 1976–1977; and former chairman of the Democratic Study Group and Americans for Democratic Action.

ROBERT A. LICHT is a research fellow at the American Enterprise Institute for Public Policy Research. He has been a National Endowment for the Humanities Fellow at AEI and a visiting scholar at the Kennedy Institute, Center for Bio-Ethics at Georgetown University, and he has taught at Bucknell University and St. John's College, Annapolis.

NELSON W. POLSBY is professor of political science at the University of California at Berkeley. His books include *Community Power and Political Theory; Congress and the Presidency; Presidential Elections,* with Aaron Wildavsky; *The Citizen's Choice: Humphrey or Nixon;* and *Political Promises.*

Selected AEI Publications

Public Opinion, published bimonthly (one year, $12; two years, $22; single copy, $2.50)

Bureaucrats, Policy Analysts, Statesmen: Who Leads? Robert A. Goldwin, ed. (134 pp., paper $5.25, cloth $10.25)

A Conversation with Gerald R. Ford: Thoughts on Economics and Politics in the 1980s (19 pp., $2.25)

A Conversation with George Bush (26 pp., $3.25)

Choosing Presidential Candidates: How Good Is the New Way? John Charles Daly, mod. (30 pp., $3.75)

The Changing British Party System, 1945-1979, S.E. Finer (264 pp., $7.25)

A Conversation with Philip M. Crane (25 pp., $2.25)

A Conversation with Vladimir Bukovsky (22 pp., $2.25)

The Denigration of Capitalism: Six Points of View, Michael Novak, ed. (64 pp., $4.25).

Church, State and Public Policy: The New Shape of the Church-State Debate, Jay Mechling, ed. (119 pp., paper $5.25, cloth $10.25)

A Conversation with Mayor Marion Barry (18 pp., $2.25)

A Conversation with Anne de Lattre: Developing the Sahel (19 pp., $2.25)

Prices subject to change without notice.

AEI Associates Program

The American Enterprise Institute invites your participation in the competition of ideas through its AEI Associates Program. This program has two objectives:

The first is to broaden the distribution of AEI studies, conferences, forums, and reviews, and thereby to extend public familiarity with the issues. AEI Associates receive regular information on AEI research and programs, and they can order publications and cassettes at a savings.

The second objective is to increase the research activity of the American Enterprise Institute and the dissemination of its published materials to policy makers, the academic community, journalists, and others who help shape public attitudes. Your contribution, which in most cases is partly tax deductible, will help ensure that decision makers have the benefit of scholarly research on the practical options to be considered before programs are formulated. The issues studied by AEI include:

- Defense Policy
- Economic Policy
- Energy Policy
- Foreign Policy
- Government Regulation
- Health Policy
- Legal Policy
- Political and Social Processes
- Social Security and Retirement Policy
- Tax Policy

For more information, write to:

American Enterprise Institute
1150 Seventeenth Street, N.W.
Washington, D.C. 20036